Andrew Johnson

Titles in the *United States Presidents* series:

United States Presidents

Andrew Johnson

Series Consultant:
Don M. Coerver, professor of history
Texas Christian University, Forth Worth, Texas

Mary Malone

Enslow Publishers, Inc.

40 Industrial Road   PO Box 38
Box 398   Aldershot
Berkeley Heights, NJ 07922   Hants GU12 6BP
USA   UK

http://www.enslow.com

Library of Congress Cataloging-in-Publication Data

Malone, Mary.
  Andrew Johnson / Mary Malone
    p. cm. — (United States presidents)
  Includes bibliographical references and index.
  Summary: A biography of the man who became President upon the
assassination of Lincoln emphasizing his turbulent White House years.
  ISBN 0-7660-1034-1
  1. Johnson, Andrew, 1808–1875—Juvenile literature.
  2. Presidents—United States—Biography—Juvenile literature.
  [1. Johnson, Andrew, 1808–1875. 2. Presidents.] I. Title.
  II. Series.
  E667.M25 1999
  973.8'1'092—dc21
  [B]   98-29560
                                                      CIP
                                                      AC

Printed in the United States of America

10 9 8 7 6 5 4 3 2 1

To Our Readers:
All Internet addresses in this book were active and appropriate when
we went to press. Any comments or suggestions can be sent by e-mail
to Comments@enslow.com or to the address on the back cover.

Illustration Credits: Andrew Johnson National Historic Site, National
Park Service, Greeneville, Tennessee, pp. 6, 26, 47, 49, 81; CORBIS-
BETTMANN, p. 45, 73; Library of Congress, pp. 9, 75, 83, 91, 94, 100, 107;
National Archives, pp. 16, 98.
All the following have been reproduced from *Dictionary of American Portraits*
(New York: Dover Publications, Inc., 1967): pp. 29, 42; Engraving by John
C. Buttre, p. 79; Photograph by Alexander Gardner, courtesy New York
Historical Society, p. 11; Retouched photograph by Matthew Brady, courtesy
U.S. Department of State, p. 115.

Source Document Credits: CORBIS-BETTMANN, pp. 67, 68, 93;
Courtesy of North Carolina Division of Archives and History,
p. 20; Illinois State Historical Library, p. 77; Library of Congress,
pp. 34, 97; National Archives, pp. 13, 102; Tennessee State Library and
Archives, pp. 54–55.

Cover Illustration: White House Collection, courtesy of the White House
Historical Association.

DEC   2000

Contents

This portrait of Johnson was taken around 1857, after he became a United States senator from Tennessee.

1

BLACK FRIDAY

V ice-President Andrew Johnson was fast asleep in his hotel room in Washington, D.C., when his friend Leonard Farwell, the former governor of Michigan, came rushing in to see him. He was bearing terrible news: President Abraham Lincoln had just been assassinated. Farwell had been in Ford's Theatre that fateful evening, April 14, 1865, when the president was shot from behind. After President Lincoln was shot, Farwell had actually seen the assassin jump to the stage and then run off.

Farwell had quickly pushed his way past the chaos in the theater and hurried to warn Johnson. He knew the vice-president was living in the Kirkwood House hotel. Earlier that day Johnson had refused Farwell's invitation to join him at the theater, saying he didn't feel well.

As soon as he reached Johnson's hotel, Farwell instructed the employees there to bar the doors and guard all the entrances. No one knew what evil schemes were afoot in Washington; the vice-president might be attacked next.

Farwell roused his friend and told him the tragic news. Farwell had seen the unconscious president being carried out of Ford's Theatre to a rooming house across the street. He was certain Lincoln was dead.

Johnson swayed from the impact of the news and staggered to a chair. He was overcome by the enormity of what he had heard. He buried his head in his hands and wept. He loved Abraham Lincoln, admired him, and believed in his lenient policies toward the South, which had just been defeated in the Civil War. In fact, Johnson owed Abraham Lincoln his very job.

As it happened, Vice-President Andrew Johnson came very close to being assassinated along with President Lincoln on what would soon become known as Black Friday, that tragic date in April 1865. Although the Civil War was officially over, the hatred stirred up by it was still strong.

John Wilkes Booth, a well-known actor, was a fanatic who wanted to avenge the defeat of the South by killing President Lincoln. He felt other leaders of the victorious North should be removed as well. With the help of a brutish crew, he planned to murder four prominent men. Besides the president, whom Booth had selected for his own personal target, the four men

In this drawing from Harper's Weekly, *actor John Wilkes Booth fires a fatal shot at President Abraham Lincoln, as he sits in his box at Ford's Theatre.*

included Vice-President Johnson, Secretary of State William Seward, and Ulysses S. Grant, general-in-chief of the Union armies. If Booth's gang had succeeded, they would have cut out the heart of the federal government.

Of the four, only President Lincoln was killed, as he sat with his wife in a box in Ford's Theatre, watching the performance of a popular play. General Grant, who had planned to attend the theater with the Lincolns, had changed his mind at the last minute and went on a trip out of town. Secretary of State Seward was in bed, recovering from a carriage accident in which his jaw had been fractured. Lewis Paine, his would-be assassin, managed to reach Seward's side and succeeded in attacking him. However, the heavy bandages on the secretary's face and neck deflected the assassin's knife, and the throat wound that was intended to be fatal eventually healed.

Vice-President Johnson's appointed assassin, George Atzerodt, had lurked outside the Kirkwood House hotel, waiting to attack Johnson when he came out. However, Atzerodt grew tired of waiting, and besides, it was well known that Johnson always carried a gun. So the appointed murderer went off instead to a tavern where he spent most of the night drinking.

In spite of Farwell's protests, Johnson insisted on getting dressed and going to the scene of the crime. Together they pushed through the riotous crowds in the street. The president was still alive, but in a deep coma,

George Atzerodt was a conspirator in the plot to kill Lincoln and other important government officials. Specifically, he was designated to assassinate Vice-President Johnson.

his brain shattered by the assassin's bullet, his life ebbing away while physicians and government leaders stood helplessly by his bedside. He had been taken from the theater to the Petersen rooming house across the street, and there laid on a bed in a first-floor bedroom. Johnson looked down sadly at the dying president. He stayed there until Mrs. Lincoln, overcome with shock, was led into the room.

Then Johnson returned to his hotel where he spent a restless night. He was awake early the next morning when Attorney General Henry Stanbery and Secretary of the Treasury Hugh McCulloch arrived, delivering the message that Abraham Lincoln had died shortly after dawn. Andrew Johnson was now president of the United States. He agreed to take the oath of office at 10 A.M. in the parlor of the Kirkwood House hotel. At that appointed time, in the presence of most of the Cabinet members and several senators, Andrew Johnson was sworn in as the seventeenth American president. He was fifty-six years old. He had been vice-president for only a little over a month.

Throughout the simple ceremony confirming him as president, Johnson's swarthy, somber face was even gloomier than usual. He seemed overwhelmed by the entire tragedy. He spoke briefly after the swearing-in, judging a long speech to be inappropriate. He merely stated that he would rely upon those present to help him carry the government through its present danger. He also declared his intention to follow President Lincoln's policies.

SOURCE DOCUMENT

SURRAT.   BOOTH.   HAROLD.

War Department, Washington, April 20, 1865,

$100,000 REWARD!

THE MURDERER

Of our late beloved President, Abraham Lincoln,

IS STILL AT LARGE.

$50,000 REWARD

Will be paid by this Department for his apprehension, in addition to any reward offered by Municipal Authorities or State Executives.

$25,000 REWARD

Will be paid for the apprehension of JOHN H. SURRATT, one of Booth's Accomplices.

$25,000 REWARD

Will be paid for the apprehension of David C. Harold, another of Booth's accomplices.

LIBERAL REWARDS will be paid for any information that shall conduce to the arrest of either of the above-named criminals, or their accomplices.

All persons harboring or secreting the said persons, or either of them, or aiding or assisting their concealment or escape, will be treated as accomplices in the murder of the President and the attempted assassination of the Secretary of State, and shall be subject to trial before a Military Commission and the punishment of DEATH.

Let the stain of innocent blood be removed from the land by the arrest and punishment of the murderers.

All good citizens are exhorted to aid public justice on this occasion. Every man should consider his own conscience charged with this solemn duty, and rest neither night nor day until it be accomplished.

EDWIN M. STANTON, Secretary of War.

DESCRIPTIONS.—BOOTH is Five Feet 7 or 8 inches high, slender build, high forehead, black hair, black eyes, and wears a heavy black moustache.

JOHN H. SURRAT is about 5 feet, 9 inches. Hair rather thin and dark; eyes rather light; no beard. Would weigh 145 or 150 pounds. Complexion rather pale and clear, with color in his cheeks. Wore light clothes of fine quality. Shoulders square; cheek bones rather prominent; chin narrow; ears projecting at the top; forehead rather low and square, but broad. Parts his hair on the right side; neck rather long. His lips are firmly set. A slim man.

DAVID C. HAROLD is five feet six inches high, hair dark, eyes dark, eyebrows rather heavy, full face, nose short, hand short and fleshy, feet small, instep high, round bodied, naturally quick and active, slightly closes his eyes when looking at a person.

NOTICE.—In addition to the above, State and other authorities have offered rewards amounting to almost one hundred thousand dollars, making an aggregate of about TWO HUNDRED THOUSAND DOLLARS.

Rewards were quickly offered for the capture of the conspirators in President Lincoln's assassination.

President Andrew Johnson was now heir to Lincoln's plans for a humanitarian restoration of the southern, Confederate states. He would be the one to preside over this nation so recently torn apart by civil war. He would have to reconcile the two sections of the country and bring them together again. The trouble was, he wasn't Abraham Lincoln. He lacked Lincoln's talents of persuasion and compromise and his saving sense of humor.

Nevertheless, Johnson was determined to carry out Lincoln's program of reconstruction, or rebuilding, for the South, which had just been so badly devastated by the Civil War. In Congress, the new president made powerful enemies, men who held different ideas. In fact, he almost lost his presidency.[1]

2

THE TAILOR'S APPRENTICE

A ndrew Johnson was born in Raleigh, North Carolina, on December 29, 1808. No president came from a more humble background, not even Abraham Lincoln. The shack where Johnson was born was no better than a log cabin, and his parents, like many poor people of the time, could not read or write. However, they were hardworking and managed to eke out a living for themselves and their two boys. Jacob Johnson, the father, was a handyman who did odd jobs in the town. His wife, Mary (Polly) McDonough Johnson, took in washing.

Andrew was only three and his older brother, William, eight when tragedy struck the family. Jacob Johnson died suddenly while ringing the town bell, one of his odd jobs. Shortly before, Johnson had rescued two of the town's prominent citizens from drowning in an icy pond. Johnson saw the men struggling in the water after their canoe had overturned; at once, he jumped into the water and pulled them safely to shore. The rescue effort, it was rumored, had weakened him.[1] Years later, when Andrew Johnson was president, the town of Raleigh placed a monument over Jacob Johnson's gravesite to commemorate his heroic deed.

The house where Johnson was born in Raleigh, North Carolina.

The Johnson family was now destitute. Mrs. Johnson struggled to raise her two sons. Without a husband, it was difficult to keep them from running wild. Even the discipline of education was denied them, as there were no free public schools then, and private education cost too much money. Andrew Johnson later claimed he never spent a single day in a schoolroom.

As soon as the boys were old enough, their mother arranged for them to be apprenticed to one of the town's tailors. William was first, then it was Andrew's turn. Being bound over to an employer would not only provide for the boys' upkeep but would also train them for jobs. Tailoring employed many men in those days, especially in the small towns that had no stores to provide ready-made clothing. Most of the men in town who could afford it had their suits, coats, and vests made to order by a tailor. The wealthier customers might select more expensive cloth and have their vests decorated with embroidery and their coats embellished with fancy buttons. All of the tailors took pride in fitting their clients with well-made, durable clothes. Later in life, Andrew Johnson still made his own clothes and was always described as being faultlessly dressed.

Andrew began his apprenticeship to James Selby the tailor when he was fourteen. The contract stated that he would not be free of this obligation until the age of twenty-one.

It was hard for a growing boy to be confined, sitting cross-legged on a tailor's bench, cutting and stitching all day long. However, Andrew discovered there was one great benefit to his job: He learned about books. It was a custom at that time for readers to come to the tailor shop and read to the employees as they worked. This was mostly a volunteer service performed by men of the town who had the leisure for it. One such person, Dr. William Hill, came regularly to read to the workers in Mr. Selby's shop. Andrew was a rapt listener. One of the books he especially enjoyed was a collection of speeches by famous orators, and he asked for repeated readings from it. A kindly man, Dr. Hill saw the boy's interest, and eventually gave him the book. By that time, Andrew had begun to read a little by himself, aided by the volunteers and some of the older workers in the shop. The shop foreman had taken a liking to Andrew and helped in his reading lessons. He called Andrew a "wild and harem-scarum youngster"[2] but noted he was always ready to learn.

Andrew learned quickly. His growing skills opened up a new world. He was impressed by the power of language, not only from the readings, but also from the conversations of customers. They discussed politics and often argued over and debated all the important topics of the times.

Although he had to work in the shop most of the day, Andrew had some free time in the evenings for a little fun. With his young friends, he roamed the town. Often the boys were boisterous and rowdy, teasing girls they knew, engaging in rough-and-tumble games. One evening they went to the home of a widow who had attractive young daughters and began throwing stones at the windows. Andrew's stone broke a window and aroused the widow. She threatened to put them in jail, and the boys ran. Andrew knew Mr. Selby would not go easy on him when he found out, so he decided to run away. Joined by his brother, he left Raleigh and walked all night to the neighboring town of Carthage.

Luckily, the boys found work in a tailor shop there. Then they learned that Mr. Selby had advertised for them, offering a reward of ten dollars for the return of the runaways. Andrew Johnson was described as "legally bound, of dark complexion, black hair and eyes, five feet, four or five inches."[3]

The runaways feared to go home and decided to travel farther. They crossed the state line and settled in Laurens, South Carolina. After a while, William left for home, but Andrew stayed in Laurens for two years, again finding work with a tailor.

When he was sixteen, he met a girl he liked named Sarah Wood whose parents made her refuse Andrew's offer of marriage. It seemed that a lowly tailor was not regarded seriously enough by the young lady's family. Andrew felt humiliated, and at the same time resentful of those who considered themselves superior to a working man like himself. He vowed to overcome poverty and discrimination and someday to face the elite on their own terms. However, he would never desert the poor, the "common people" from whom he had sprung.

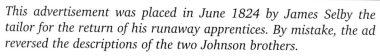

SOURCE DOCUMENT

Ten Dollars Reward.

RAN AWAY from the Subscriber, on the night of the 15th instant, two apprentice boys, legally bound, named WILLIAM and AN DREW JOHNSON The former is of a dark complexion, black hair, eyes, and habits. They are much of a height, about 5 feet 4 or 5 inches The latter is very fleshy, freckled face, light hair, and fair complexion. They went off with two other apprentices, advertised by Messrs Wm. & Chas. Fowler When they went away, they were well clad—blue cloth coats, light colored homespun coats, and new hats, the maker's name in the crown of the hats, is Theodore Clark. I will pay the above Reward to any person who will deliver said apprentices to me in Raleigh, or I will give the above Reward for Andrew Johnson alone.

All persons are cautioned against harboring or employing said apprentices, on pain of being prosecuted.

JAMES J. SELBY, Tailor.
Raleigh, N. C. June 24, 1824   26 3t

This advertisement was placed in June 1824 by James Selby the tailor for the return of his runaway apprentices. By mistake, the ad reversed the descriptions of the two Johnson brothers.

Soon Andrew began to regret shirking his duty, so he returned to Raleigh. Andrew had hoped that by now Mr. Selby might forgive and reemploy him. However, Mr. Selby would not take him back, nor would he release Andrew from his contract. Under such a cloud, no one else in town could employ him, either. So Andrew left town again, this time alone.

He hiked across the Appalachian Mountains, hitching his way on the wagons of any drivers who would stop for him. He arrived in Knoxville, Tennessee, then went by flatboat to Decatur, Georgia, then walked seventy miles across country to Columbia, South Carolina. Again he found employment with a town tailor, James Shelton. His stay in Columbia was pleasant. The Sheltons treated him kindly, and Mrs. Shelton later claimed to have taught him to read. Asked about that claim when he was president, Andrew Johnson said, "She did not, but she seemed to get so much pleasure out of saying that she did, that I have not denied it. I am glad to give her all the pleasure that I can, for she was a mother to me when I lived with them and worked at my trade with her husband."[4]

After six months in Columbia, Andrew met some people from Raleigh and learned that his mother was again destitute. Her marriage to another poor man named Turner Doughtry had worsened her condition instead of improving it. Andrew's brother, William, had left Raleigh for work on an uncle's farm in Tennessee.

So, Andrew returned home over the long, hard trail that took him back to Raleigh.

Arriving home, Andrew realized that he was now the head of his small family. After assessing the situation, he decided that all three of them—his mother, his step-father, and himself—should leave Raleigh and follow William to Tennessee. He hoped they would find honest work there and be treated with respect.

The family gathered their battered possessions and set out leading a two-wheeled cart pulled by a blind pony. They took turns riding in the pony cart and walk-ing. They planned to stop first at the uncle's farm in east Tennessee where William was living, but they never reached it. Travel was slow and sometimes dangerous. Often they evaded wild creatures that had to be scared off by the sound of Andrew's shotgun. Crossing the mountains was difficult, as was enduring the dust, heat, and storms that they encountered along the way.

After several days, the family arrived in east Tennessee, in the foothills of the Great Smoky Mountains. They did not know the name of the town spread out below, but it looked so peaceful and protect-ed that they felt they wanted to stop there—at least for a time. As it turned out, the Johnson party wound up staying for good. Greeneville would become Andrew Johnson's home, his workplace, and the starting point for his political career.

3

AT HOME IN GREENEVILLE

Many myths about our presidents have been entwined with the facts of their lives. Some stories are true, or partially true. Others are popular and have become part of the presidential folklore. One story about Andrew Johnson relates how he and his future wife first met on a late summer day in 1826, when he was only seventeen.

Arriving in the town of Greeneville for the first time from the mountain trail he and his family had been following for many days, Andrew noticed an attractive young woman standing outside a well-kept house. She did not recoil from the sight of the ragged group. In fact, she looked so kind that Andrew asked the young woman if she knew of an empty house or cabin where they could find shelter in town. She told him that a

23

storekeeper, Mr. Armitage, had an empty cabin on his property, and she pointed the way to his store.

Andrew found Mr. Armitage willing to let the weary travelers stay in his cabin for a few days. When he learned that Andrew knew the tailor's craft, he extended this time so that Andrew could cut and stitch a quantity of homespun cloth into garments. Mr. Armitage informed Andrew that the town tailor was growing old and was close to retirement. In the weeks following, the Johnsons found a small cabin to rent, and Andrew completed his work for Mr. Armitage.

The story goes that Eliza McCardle, the young woman who directed Andrew to the storekeeper, seeing beyond his shabby appearance, decided that he was the man she was going to marry. She even told her girl-friends, who teased her about her new beau.

How the two met after this first encounter is not recorded, but they did marry a year later. He was eighteen, she was sixteen. As it turned out, his marriage to Eliza was fortunate for Andrew Johnson. She was not only attractive, but intelligent and well educated, according to the standards of the time, having completed an elementary education. At once Eliza began to teach Andrew to write and to do arithmetic. After learning the alphabet, he proceeded rapidly to writing his own name. Putting down his ideas into words was thrilling for Andrew. As for reading, he was doing so well that books became his most prized possessions.

The old tailor in Greeneville retired soon after

Andrew's arrival there. The young couple moved into a two-room house on Main Street and opened shop. The front room became the tailor shop and the back one the Johnsons' family room—a combined parlor, kitchen, and bedroom. During the next two years, it also became the birthplace of the Johnsons' first two children, Martha and Charles.

The tailor shop prospered. Johnson's skill—he had learned his trade well—was soon recognized in Greeneville. He liked the town and the people. Even the wealthy elite of the town came to him because he gave good value and made exceptional, well-fitting apparel. Eventually, "every judge, lawyer, parson, doctor, embalmer and storekeeper in the Greeneville area went to Andy Johnson for his clothes."[1]

As time went on, Johnson hired helpers to assist him and paid readers seven cents an hour to read to his workers. Books were Johnson's education. Hungry for learning, he took from great books what he had missed in formal schooling. In later public life, although he would usually criticize the government for spending money on some internal improvements like roads and railways, he was always ready to spend money on libraries and schools.

Johnson's skill in tailoring was not the only attraction that drew people to his shop. His growing interest in political affairs became well known, and he aligned himself with the laborers—farmers, workmen, and mechanics. He called himself a "plebeian," one of the

Johnson's first tailor shop, now part of the Andrew Johnson National Historic Site in Greeneville, Tennessee.

common people, and he was proud of it. He despised the wealthy, slave-holding plantation class that ruled the South, although in east Tennessee, where Greeneville was located, there were fewer plantations and fewer slaves than in other parts of the South.

There were two colleges near Greeneville. Andrew Johnson soon became familiar with their courses and arranged to sit in on many of the lectures. Every evening he walked to one college or the other, and sometimes he even took part in their debates. The college students welcomed his opinions and respected them. In those days, at that place, theatrical entertainment was very rare. Debates between opposing groups took the place of theater. Soon, in Johnson's shop, debates were carried on in an informal way. His friends started a political club there, and Johnson soon realized he had a natural gift for speechmaking. He and a few close friends who shared his opinions and populist policies became a tight-knit group. Among them were some who became lifelong supporters—Mordecai Lincoln, a tanner and cousin of Abraham Lincoln's; Blackston McDaniel, a plasterer; and Sam Milligan, a teacher at Greeneville College, who became Johnson's political and legal adviser. They talked politics well into every night.

One day in 1828, as a prank, the four friends put their names up for election to the town council. Until then, it had always been wealthy, upper-class men who were elected to the council. This time, however, to the surprise of the old council members and the four themselves, they were all elected to the seven-man town council. In addition, they were reelected for the next two years. Then, in 1830, his friends convinced Johnson to run for mayor of Greeneville. He did not need much convincing—politics had entered his blood. When he won the election, he considered it a victory for the common people over the elite. To add to this impressive accomplishment, Johnson was elected a trustee to the Rhea Academy, a secondary school in the area. For a man who had never spent a day in a classroom, this was sweet revenge on all the people who had looked down on the humble tailor.

Johnson's prosperous tailor shop enabled him to save some money, and he invested wisely in property around Greeneville. His land included a farm where he installed his mother and stepfather. In 1831, he moved his own growing family to a bigger house with more room for the children, which soon included another daughter, Mary, and another son, Robert.

Andrew Johnson was mayor of Greeneville for more than three years. Then, in 1835, a chance came for him to enter the realm of state politics. The position he sought was representative to the Tennessee state legislature. Although his sympathies were with the Democratic party, he was an independent in his first political campaign.

In those days the two chief political parties in the South were the Whigs and the Democrats. The Whigs were the forerunners of today's Republican party. They believed in a strong federal government. They stood for a national bank, a high tariff or tax on foreign imports, and expansion of roads and canals. The Democrats were divided on these issues and believed in states' rights first. The Democrats' hero was former president Andrew Jackson, the champion of the common people. Jackson was also Andrew Johnson's personal hero, as well as his namesake.

Johnson ran as a Jacksonian Democrat. He was a tireless candidate, and his speechmaking, although rough, was powerful. He could be loud, sarcastic, scornful, and bruising to his opponents. The people—the common people—loved his style. His forceful words

Former president Andrew Jackson, who had also been active in Tennessee state politics, was Johnson's personal hero, as well as his namesake.

were entertaining, and they regularly swayed listeners to his side.

Going into the campaign, virtually unknown in the adjoining county, the odds were against him. However, Johnson won the election and a seat in the state legislature. He was triumphant; politics was clearly his calling. Now he became known as the "tailor turned politician."[2]

4

TAILOR TURNED POLITICIAN

In 1835, at the age of twenty-seven, Andrew Johnson traveled to the Tennessee state legislature in Nashville, one hundred miles from Greeneville. Nashville had notable public buildings, stores, banks, and churches. Compared to sleepy Greeneville, it was a bustling city.

In those days, the legislative sessions were fairly short, and the representatives could return home during recess to resume their regular jobs. The young legislator from Greene and Washington counties had leased his tailor shop temporarily. However, he kept the sign over it that read "A. Johnson Tailor." That sign would never come down. It was his pride and the symbol of his plebeian status.

In Nashville, Johnson roomed with a Whig friend,

John Netherland. He made other friends in the Whig party. In fact, his party affiliation was not yet firm. But he often spoke out against the Whig proposals to extend the railroad system to adjoining states. Johnson also called for economy in government and fewer laws. However, when he returned home, he found that many people in his counties were angry with him. They opposed his voting against their interests in the expansion of the railroads and against raising state workers' salaries. When election time came around again, Johnson was defeated. It was the only time he was to lose an election until after the Civil War.[1]

Johnson was stung by the criticism at home. He vowed to stick with the Democratic party of former president Andrew Jackson from then on. His reputation as a fiery fighter for the populist cause spread throughout east Tennessee. He campaigned nonstop and made many speeches. His voice and passion helped make him popular. To his opposition, he was slashing and offensive, and that, too, made him popular. His real followers, the poor, the working class, the mountain people, the mechanics, the artisans and craftsmen, loved him and his style. He was straightforward and not afraid to deliver insults and scathing critiques. He became known as a "stump speaker" who would speak everywhere and anywhere, even on a tree stump if no other platform was available.

Because he had enemies who often threatened him, Johnson started to carry a gun, and he made sure his listeners could see it. Always a man of the people, he was referred to by his faithful supporters as "Andy" Johnson. This time, after a lively campaign, he was reelected to the legislature in 1839.

In 1840, the governorship of Tennessee was won by fellow Democrat James K. Polk, and Andrew Johnson decided to aim for the state senate. He won election in 1841. While in office he continued his opposition to the Whigs' support of a national bank, a high tariff, and internal improvements like roads and canals. However, most of his resolutions failed to pass the Whig majority in the senate. One of them was to discontinue opening the legislative sessions with prayers. Although Johnson believed in religious toleration, he himself belonged to no Church and upheld no specific religion. His wife, Eliza, and their oldest child, Martha, belonged to the Methodist Church, but they could not persuade Johnson to join them. His own religion was based on the Bible, one of the first books he had read thoroughly, and on the Constitution of the United States, to which he was devoted. He interpreted the Constitution strictly, that is, reading no more into it than its exact words denoted. His icon was the American flag.

Andrew Johnson's personal fortune grew as well as his political success. His family was now financially well-off, living in a bigger, more comfortable house near his tailor shop, which he continued to run. He employed several tailors, and even owned a few slaves for household work.

Johnson was a firm believer in the provisions of the United States Constitution. He interpreted the document strictly, reading into it only what its exact words denoted.

Although there were fewer slaves in Tennessee than in the deep South, Andrew Johnson, like most of the white people there, upheld slavery. In their view, the economy of the South depended on the slave system, and the Constitution allowed it. That document guaranteed the right to hold property, and slaves were property, Johnson believed.[2] He was never against slavery as long as it was constitutional. He put the Union first, and said at one time that he was for the Union with slavery or without slavery.[3]

Johnson continued to read constantly. When his daughter Martha started school, Senator Johnson was not ashamed to learn along with her from the textbooks she brought home. He became acquainted with the great books of his time, especially those related to politics and history. He subscribed to every newspaper and periodical printed in his district, whether it was for or against his beliefs. When reading aloud he sometimes mispronounced words, and his spelling, when he wrote letters and notes, was not always perfect.

Johnson felt he could never make up for the lack of an early education. Most of his fellow legislators were trained lawyers, equipped with the basic education he had never been able to pursue, the lack of which he still sorely regretted.

However, Johnson's family life was happy. Eliza was a constant source of loyalty and support. Her calm and quiet way was often in sharp contrast to his passion and fire. When he became agitated about some wrong or slur, she would merely put her hand on his shoulder and murmur, "Andrew, Andrew." Eliza's gentle voice and touch always worked to calm her husband. Johnson's two daughters and his wife were his most loyal supporters. He would always listen to their suggestions and pay more attention to their advice than to any of his political advisers.

As the champion of the working class, Andrew Johnson spoke out often against the aristocratic, slave-holding society that ruled the South. He despised their lordly behavior, the way they looked down on people like himself. While he was in the state legislature, he tried to lessen the power of this wealthy class.

In voting for representation in the legislature, the plantation owners were allowed to count three fifths of their slaves, who, of course, could not vote themselves. This increased the owners' overall number, which gave them the right to more representatives. Johnson proposed to abolish this practice. His action outraged the ruling class and was quickly put down by other legislators. Johnson's motive in trying to abolish the three-fifths rule was not to help the slaves. He was not an abolitionist—someone who wanted to end slavery. Indeed, his attitude toward slavery remained the same. As always, he believed in white supremacy and the inferiority of the black race. He was simply concerned for the poor whites who owned no land or farms and had to do the hard work of the nation. With this proposal, Johnson tried to lessen the plantation owners' power.

Johnson wanted Knoxville in east Tennessee to become the state capital, but he lost that bid, and in 1843, Nashville was voted in. He even suggested that it would be a good idea to make east Tennessee a separate state, along with some territory from adjoining states whose interests were similar to east Tennessee's. That proposal, too, was quickly killed.

Johnson continued to oppose the policies of the Whigs. He won an interesting fight against them in 1841. It was the job of the Tennessee state legislature, in joint session with the state senate, to vote for two senators for the United States Senate. Two vacancies opened up close together. The Whigs had a majority of only one in the joint legislature at that time, but they could still outvote the Democrats and thus win both United States Senate positions. The Whigs refused any compromise that would give one vacancy to the Democrats. Accordingly, under Johnson's leadership, it was decided there would be no vote at all, and therefore, no victory for the Whigs. The Democrats refused to allow a vote to come up on the subject, thus imposing a deadlock on the issue that lasted throughout the entire session of the legislature. It was a bold ploy, but it worked. For two years, Tennessee had no United States senators. The maneuver pleased the Democratic leadership in both the state and the nation. Governor Polk praised Johnson's strategy, and so did "Old Hickory" himself, former president Andrew Jackson.

Now there was talk about sending Andy Johnson to

Washington. To his faithful followers, he was a dominant political figure. His speeches were compelling, and in person he presented a dignified style. Just above average in height, he was always well dressed. His jet-black hair and dark piercing eyes, swarthy complexion, and stern, sometimes grim expression made a striking impression. Johnson looked like a man who had fought his way up. Above all, he was known for his honesty and his refusal to soften his words to suit others, regardless of the effect on his own political career. He never went against his supporters. His popularity was so great among the common people of east Tennessee that it was said, "he was stronger than the party itself."[4]

Andrew Johnson was ready for higher office. In 1843, he announced that he was a candidate from his district for the United States House of Representatives.

5

ON THE NATIONAL SCENE

A fter having served in both the state legislature and state senate for a combination of six years, Andrew Johnson was elected the United States congressman from his Tennessee district. This position was his first step into national politics. He was backed by good friends in Greeneville, especially those of the tailor shop crowd who had been with him from the beginning, his loyal supporters as well as advisers.

Johnson had become widely known throughout Tennessee as the "tailor-politician" and as an electrifying stump speaker. He usually demolished the candidates in the Whig party who had the courage to challenge him. One who tried, Judge Oliver Temple, although beaten by Johnson, could not help being impressed by the tailor-politician's force. Judge Temple declared that "upon the stump, Johnson never met his match."[1] His voice seemed especially suitable for speaking in the open air. It was always clear and ringing, pleasant to the ear. He sprinkled his words with many references to the Bible as well as to the other great books he continued to read.

One of Johnson's first disappointments when he arrived in Washington, D.C., in 1843 was the large number of lawyers in Congress. He deplored that imbalance. He would have preferred more mechanics—laboring people—as legislators.

Congressman Johnson, like most other members of Congress, lived in a boarding house near Capitol Hill. He spent much of his free time in the Library of Congress reading and enjoyed the privilege of borrowing.

Before coming to Washington, Johnson had enrolled his daughter Martha, then fifteen, in a well-recommended private school in that city. Now, thanks to his thriving business in Greeneville and some shrewd real estate investments, he was able to afford private schools for all his children. He took walks and trips around Washington with Martha, and after 1845, when Tennessee's James K. Polk became president, she was often invited to the White House. The Polks had no children of their own and took a special interest in the children of the congressmen from their home state. Martha Johnson became a favorite of Mrs. Polk's and learned a great deal about White House ceremonies, often assisting in the receptions there.

Among the many congressmen that Andrew Johnson came to know, several, like himself, would become famous. Among those who served with him in those early years in Congress were ex-president John Quincy Adams from Massachusetts; Jefferson Davis from Mississippi, who would become the Confederacy's president during the Civil War; and Abraham Lincoln, congressman from Illinois.

It was not long before Andrew Johnson, populist, and Jefferson Davis, aristocrat, clashed in the House of Representatives. In one proposal, Davis requested more money for West Point, the military college from which he had graduated. Johnson opposed any plan that would give the military more power and might even encourage the formation of a standing army. In Congress, Jefferson Davis confronted him, stating that a blacksmith or a tailor could never do the work of a trained military man. Johnson responded angrily to this belittling mention of "tailor." He declared his contempt for "a swaggering scrub aristocracy who assume[d] to know a great deal . . . but possesses neither talents nor information."[2]

He and Jefferson Davis never became friendly, although they both belonged to the Democratic party. They disagreed often. Years later, when Davis was a prisoner of war and Johnson was president, the Confederate leader was asked his opinion of Andrew Johnson. He said he respected Johnson's "ability, integrity and great original force of character . . . his temperance, industry, courage and unswerving perseverance."[3]

Jefferson Davis, above, and Johnson clashed often in the House of Representatives. Davis, an aristocrat, who later became president of the Confederate states during the Civil War, looked down on Johnson's humble background.

However, he also said Johnson was "almost morbidly sensitive . . . held prejudices and preconceptions . . . which no arguments could change . . . one of the people by birth, he remained so by conviction."[4]

Andrew Johnson served in the United States Congress for ten years, from 1843 to 1853. In 1846, he introduced a bill he had long favored, the Homestead Act, which would give free land in the western territories to poor citizens who owned no homes or farms. "Free Land for Free Labor" and "Free Soil for Free Men" were the cries of the bill's supporters. Although it passed in the House of Representatives, the bill was defeated in the Senate. Nevertheless, Johnson, as its champion, won national recognition. However, his reputation in the South suffered. The plantation-based aristocracy opposed the idea of free land for free people. That proposal would abolish, or end, slavery, they feared. Many southerners also suspected Johnson of supporting the abolitionists of the North who had long spoken out for the complete abolition of slavery.

Their suspicions were far from true. Johnson was certainly not opposed to slavery. He continued to believe the Constitution protected that institution, and he upheld the return of fugitive slaves to their owners. The poor whites who supported Johnson agreed with his position. They believed—rightly or not—that if the abolitionists had their way, freed slaves would be turned loose on the South, and the whites, far outnumbered, would be exterminated. In that view, setting the

Negroes free would be as great an evil as the abolitionists claimed for slavery itself. With the slaveholders dominating the South, the Homestead Act never passed in Johnson's many successive terms in the House of Representatives.

Johnson kept winning reelection to his congressional seat every two years. Finally, in 1852, after his fifth term, he found that the Whig-controlled Tennessee legislature had decided to stop him. They enlarged Johnson's district, Greene County, by attaching it to another, Whig-dominated district. In this way, they managed to lessen Johnson's support and kill his chances of reelection. At first he was depressed by this turn of events and briefly considered retirement from politics, but in the fall of 1852, urged on by his supporters, Johnson decided to run for governor of Tennessee.

He was the unanimous choice of the Democrats, and won election by the people in 1853. He was forty-five when he became the "Mechanic Governor" of Tennessee, the nickname referring to his dedication to the working people. Although many of the wealthy slave owners in the Democratic party were opposed to him, one of his followers said that Johnson "beat the Whig party as well as the leaders of the Democratic party. The masses have done the work, the mechanic[s], the day laborer[s], have come to the rescue."[5]

However, Johnson could not put through many of his proposed economies and reforms because the Whigs and the anti-Johnson forces in the legislature were

Andrew Johnson was forty-five years old when he became known as the "Mechanic Governor" of Tennessee. The nickname refers to his dedication to the working people.

against him. He did succeed in getting laws passed establishing public schools and colleges, and starting public libraries. It was his lifelong ambition to give these benefits to the people, especially the poor. He was reelected governor and served for a second term.

Back in Greeneville in August 1852, Eliza Johnson gave birth to the Johnsons' third son. He was named Andrew, Jr. but was always called Frank. So much younger than the other children, he became the pet of the family. That same year Johnson moved his family into a fine new brick house on an acre of land on Main Street in Greeneville. This would be their final home, their "homestead." It was spacious and comfortable, with verandas, a garden, and a spring of fine, clear water behind the house. Johnson opened the spring to the public, via a brick pathway from Water Street. A small building that served as his office and a meeting place for his friends was also located on the property.

A few years later, the two Johnson daughters married and established their own homes near Greeneville. Martha married David Patterson, a circuit judge; and Mary married Colonel Dan Stover. Both men were friends of Andrew Johnson.

The Johnsons' two older sons, Charles and Robert, had been given the best possible education. They tried different occupations, but did not stick to any for long. Neither one had inherited his father's drive or ambition. They were convivial, good-looking young men, but unfortunately both became addicted to alcohol. They

Andrew Johnson, Jr., the president's third and youngest son, was always called Frank.

were a constant source of worry to their parents. Johnson's concern about his sons was often revealed in his letters to his daughters, especially to Martha, his steadfast supporter and best friend. Many people thought she most resembled her father. She and her husband had two children, and the Stovers had three. Their families remained close to Andrew and Eliza Johnson, and the grandchildren became a source of great joy and comfort to them.

Governor Johnson's two terms, threatened always by the Whig-leaning majorities in the legislature, came to an end in 1857. He decided not to run for a third term. "I would prefer changing positions and now is the time to do it,"[6] he said. There was a vacancy for the position of United States senator from Tennessee. Johnson campaigned for it, and was elected. When that happened, he claimed he had "reached the summit of [his] ambition."[7]

Although Johnson had, earlier in his career, boasted, "I am no party man, bound by no party or platform and [I] will vote as I please,"[8] he was more disciplined now. His writing and spelling skills had improved, and he was not as sensitive to criticism and what he considered personal insults against his poverty-stricken youth and his early occupation.

Back in Washington, D.C., Johnson met his old opponent, Jefferson Davis, who was now a senator from Mississippi. The two would clash often in the Senate as they had in the past, and, once in a while, they would agree on something.

Martha Johnson Patterson was Johnson's older daughter and most loyal supporter.

In the Senate, Johnson was named chairman of a committee on cutting government expenses. He voted against building the Pacific Railroad. Although he had always been against railroad expansion, he did often travel on the trains, which expanded in spite of his opposition. Once on a trip he took as governor, from Memphis to Washington, the train derailed and rolled down a cliff. Johnson's right arm was badly broken in the accident. He could not use it for several months. His handwriting, so painfully learned, suffered.

He was happy when, in 1860, the Homestead Act finally seemed about to pass. It cleared both the House and the Senate. The Free Soilers were joyful. All the bill needed was the signature of the Democratic president, James Buchanan. However, the president did something almost unheard of up to that time. He vetoed the bill. Johnson was outraged. He had thought Buchanan favored the bill. When the Senate failed to override the veto, Johnson declared that the president had sold out to the "slavocracy,"[9] or slave aristocracy, which wanted to protect and preserve slavery. Johnson's hopes for the common people were dashed again. He declared that the Homestead Act was the goal of his ambition and when it passed, "he would die content."[10]

However, something even bigger than "Free Soil for Free Men" would soon expand the scope of his ambition. It was the Civil War.

6

TOWARD CIVIL WAR

A ndrew Johnson served in the Senate from 1857 to 1862. Slowly but surely during that time the country moved toward civil war. The two sides—the North and the South—held firmly to their opposing convictions.

The North, which had a short agricultural growing season, grew dependent on industry and factories to fuel its economy. Industries used machines to do their work. Although people were needed to tend the machines, not so many hands were needed as in agricultural labor. The northern states hired cheap labor to work in the factories.

In the South, there was a long growing season. The economy was primarily agricultural, based on the production and sale of crops. Growing food, grain, cotton, and tobacco is labor-intensive. Many people are needed to harvest and store the crops. The South grew dependent on slaves to do this work.

There was no talk of concessions between the two sides, only fierce arguments about the two big topics—slavery and secession. The southern states were threatening to secede, or break away from the Union, if the North continued to press the issue of abolishing slavery.

All of the compromises that attempted to deal with the issue of slavery had failed. Senator Andrew Johnson said that "Compromise has been a continual and increasing source of agitation."[1] One of these compromises, the Kansas-Nebraska Act, passed in 1854, allowed for slavery in the new lands to the west, if the settlers wanted it. That policy pleased neither side, not even the South, even though it canceled the old Missouri Compromise of 1820, which forbade slavery to be extended beyond the boundaries established that year.

Now, in 1860, Jefferson Davis, speaking for the South, demanded federal protection for slavery in any new territories to be opened. The antislavery North, enraged by the controversy, formed a new party, the Republicans. Their candidate for president that year was Abraham Lincoln. He believed slavery was morally wrong. In addition, Lincoln warned that the conflict over the issue of slavery would seriously harm the nation. Lincoln pleaded that slavery should be done away with because "a house divided against itself cannot stand . . . this government cannot endure permanently half slave and half free."[2]

The presidential election of 1860 was crucial. If Lincoln were elected, some of the southern states threatened to secede from the Union. The Democratic party was split. Most of the South was Democratic. Many in the North also belonged to that party. However, now there were two factions, or parts, to the Democratic party, and both factions were running against Lincoln. Stephen Douglas represented the northern Democrats and John Breckinridge the southern wing. Although Johnson voted with the southern Democrats, he was also a Unionist, strongly against secession. He called those who wanted to secede from the Union "traitors" against the federal government. His opinion was praised in the North, but in the South only by the remainder of the old Whig party that stood for the Union. That party was now fading away, outnumbered by the Democrats. Johnson was insulted and threatened by the secessionist Democrats, even in parts of his own state.

Lincoln and his vice-president, Hannibal Hamlin, were elected in November 1860. It was easier for the Republicans to win with the Democratic votes divided into two wings. South Carolina immediately seceded. Within a few months after Lincoln's inauguration in April 1861, Mississippi, Florida, Louisiana, Alabama, and Georgia followed South Carolina's example. The senators from those states then left the Senate. Andrew Johnson had no intention of leaving the Senate.

SOURCE DOCUMENT

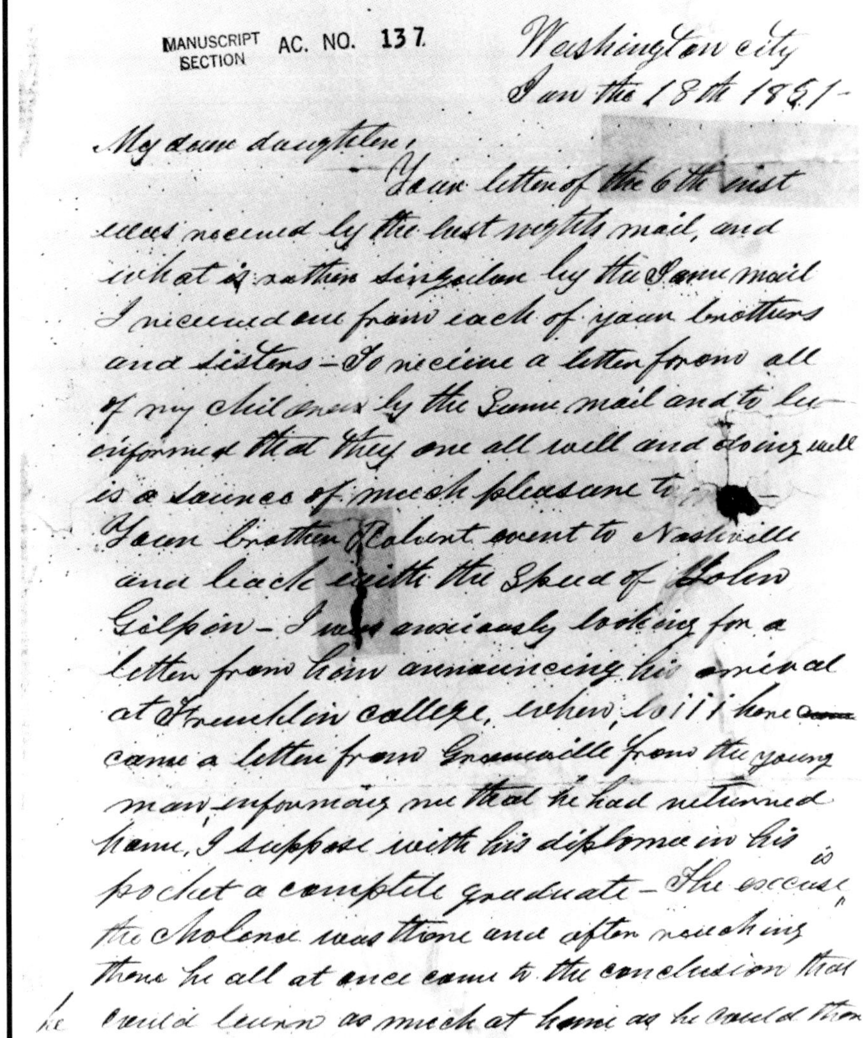

MANUSCRIPT AC. NO. **13 7.**
SECTION

[handwritten letter]

Washington City
Jan the 18th 1851 –

My dear daughter,

Your letter of the 6th inst was received by the last nights mail, and what is rather singular by the Same mail I received one from each of your brothers and sisters – To receive a letter from all of my children by the Same mail and to be informed that they are all well and doing well is a source of much pleasure to — Your brother Robert went to Nashville and back with the Speed of John Gilpin – I was anxiously looking for a letter from him announcing his arrival at Franklin College, when, lo ! ! ! here came a letter from Greeneville from the young man informing me that he had returned home, I suppose with his diploma in his pocket a complete graduate – The excuse the Cholera was there and after reaching there he all at once came to the conclusion that he could learn as much at home as he could there

This letter from Johnson to his daughter Mary was written while he was still in the United States Senate.

a very fortunate conclusion his mind happens
to come to after three hundred miles _ This will
do I think will to please him about for
same time _ After your letter came I had one
night hearty laugh over some of your nonsense _
After all it is the best way for any one to write
about things Just as they are and call them
by their broken names _ I have little or nothing
to write about at this time _ The book you request
me to buy for you I will get in a few days
and send it to you _

Give my respects to Virginia
and Miss Davidson &c _
Your father
Andrew Johnson
Miss Mary Johnson

Eventually, after more states had seceded, he would be the only southern senator left in the United States Senate, the only southern senator who refused to secede with his state.

Federal arsenals, or storehouses of ammunition, in the southern states were taken over by the rebel soldiers, usually without opposition in the face of armed power. Only Fort Sumter, in Charleston, South Carolina, resisted. The fort was fired upon and, after a forced surrender, occupied by the rebels. The Civil War had officially begun. President Lincoln then called for volunteers to join the Union Army. That act spurred on the last southern states—Virginia, North Carolina, Arkansas, and Tennessee—to secede. There would be eleven in all. They formed a new government called the Confederate States of America and elected Jefferson Davis their president.

Before Tennessee seceded, Governor Isham Harris called on the state legislature to take the state out of the Union. Some of Andrew Johnson's friends wanted him to return to east Tennessee and fight for his avowed cause—to keep Tennessee in the Union. Other friends warned him against coming back to Tennessee because of the dangers he would undoubtedly face. He left Washington anyhow, but not before making a rousing speech in the Senate against secession.

When Johnson left for Greeneville, he was accompanied by Eliza who had gone to Washington to lend her husband moral support while he was still in the

Senate. Their journey home was perilous. At one train stop, at the border between Virginia and Tennessee, a crowd bent on lynching, or killing, Johnson approached his train. He faced his enemies, standing on the train platform with his revolver drawn. Pressed back by Johnson's determined, fearless look, the crowd held off, and the train continued on its way. A telegraph message then came from Jefferson Davis stationed at his Confederate headquarters in Richmond, Virginia. It warned the trainmen not to stop at Bristol, Virginia, because a mob was waiting for Johnson. Members of the Johnson party believed the message from Davis was meant to prevent Johnson's murder, which would have made him a martyr to the Union cause.

There were enemies even in Greeneville, but that did not stop Johnson from going about stumping all over east Tennessee, trying to persuade people to keep their state in the Union. A vote was finally held, and showed overwhelming support statewide for secession. However, in east Tennessee, Andrew Johnson's home territory, the vote was against secession by two to one. His own region had voted to stay with the Union. That prompted Johnson to say that the people had never deserted him and he, in turn, would never desert them.[3] Of course, the amount of people in his own district was not enough to prevent Tennessee from following the other seceded states.

With Tennessee now part of the Confederacy, Johnson had to flee for his life. The Tennessee militia had orders to arrest him as a traitor. First, he arranged for his wife and young son to go to the home of the Johnsons' daughter Martha Patterson. Later on, they moved to second daughter Mary Stover's farm in Carter County. Eliza Johnson, in poor health since the birth of Andrew, Jr., was now being treated for early signs of tuberculosis.

The Johnsons' two older sons, both ardent Unionists like their father, were with Dan Stover, Mary's husband, who was scouting in the mountains.

Surviving a dangerous journey, Johnson and a few loyal friends arrived safely in neutral Kentucky. From there, he traveled on to Washington, D.C., and back to the Senate.

Shortly after Johnson left Greeneville, the town fell into the hands of the Confederates. Marching into the town, they seized everything that belonged to Johnson, his family, and their friends. Soon the family home was taken over by the rebel army and used as a hospital for Confederate soldiers.

The only communication Johnson maintained with his family during the early war years was through letters, which were often delayed for weeks, and messages smuggled out by friends. It would be a long time before he saw his family again and even longer—eight years—before he saw his home.

7

MILITARY GOVERNOR

B ack in Washington, in the Senate, Johnson again took up the cause he had so long supported. The Homestead Act finally passed, with no southern legislators present to vote against it, and was signed by President Lincoln.

When Congress adjourned for the summer of 1862, Johnson received many invitations from friends in Washington to stay with them. They knew he could not safely return home to Greeneville. However, he decided it would be better to go on speaking tours to the border states—Kentucky, Missouri, West Virginia. The North wanted to keep those states in the Union. He also worked especially hard for his own state, trying to raise money, supplies, and volunteers for the defense of Tennessee against the superior Confederate forces.

Tennessee was already being torn apart by the fighting between the rebel and Union factions.

In the early engagements of the war, the Union Army failed to rout the Confederates. Those early Union defeats shocked the North. Even President Lincoln could not get the Union forces under General George McClellan to move into battle and engage the enemy. The Confederates had swiftly taken over Richmond as their capital and posed a serious threat to Washington, D.C.

In the Senate, Johnson made many speeches. Leading Republicans in Congress, like Thaddeus Stevens in the House of Representatives and Charles Sumner in the Senate, spoke, too, but more violently. They were already known as Radicals because of their strong opposition to slavery. They wanted to put down the Confederate rebels by force and, as Thaddeus Stevens said, make them sue for mercy—no bargaining, no negotiation, no truces.[1]

Johnson's speeches reflected his desire to preserve the Constitution, the laws, and the Union. He received encouraging responses from some newspaper editorials and from the public. Like Lincoln, he did not speak of revenge and retribution, about hanging all the rebels. He had compassion for the people, especially the poor whites of the South.

Not until Ulysses S. Grant was put in supreme command of the Union Army were the Confederates gradually routed from their strongholds. When Union troops were able to enter the capital city of Nashville,

Tennessee, previously held by rebel forces, President Lincoln acted. He appointed Andrew Johnson military governor of Tennessee, an unusual position created to give Johnson both civil and military authority. Lincoln hoped Johnson would help organize the loyal Unionists, hold free elections, and restore federal authority in the state. This would be a more difficult job than Lincoln or even Johnson could have foreseen.

The Confederates still held most of Tennessee, and battles with the Union troops were constant. Next to Virginia, Tennessee would have the largest number of battles fought in the Civil War. Nevertheless, Johnson accepted Lincoln's appointment as military governor and the commission as a brigadier general, and left at once for Nashville. He was accompanied by two aides and a secretary. He knew that even if he succeeded in keeping Nashville from being recaptured by the rebels, he would still be hated by most of the people in Tennessee who called him a traitor to the South.

Despite reported plots to kidnap him along the way to Nashville, Johnson managed to evade ambush and sudden attacks. When he finally reached Nashville, he found chaos in the city that was once so beautiful. Most of the leading citizens, as well as the Confederate legislature and the governor, had fled before the Union forces arrived.

Johnson was now not only military governor of an embattled state, but also dictator, judge, and jailer of wrongdoers who still hated him. He was also commander of a military force that resented his authority. General Don Carlos Buell, whose Union troops were defending Nashville, was not the most effective defender against the rebels. Fighting was still raging nearby. When a Confederate band approached and ringed the city, cutting off supplies to those within, Johnson issued a warning. Rather than let Nashville be taken, he vowed he would burn it to the ground. He also warned that at the first shot fired against the city, he would personally see to it that the Nashville houses of prominent secessionists would be demolished.

Knowing that Andrew Johnson was a man of his word, some of the citizens who had homes in the city implored the Confederate general, Nathan Bedford Forrest, not to try to take Nashville. Forrest pulled back, and for a time, Nashville was saved. The Stars and Stripes still waved over the city. That flag would continue to fly as long as Andrew Johnson was nearby.

At one point in the long siege, General Buell decided to march north four hundred miles to defend Louisville, Kentucky. He advised Johnson to evacuate Nashville. Johnson was outraged. He reminded Buell he was supposed to be defending Nashville, not Louisville. As military governor, Johnson vowed to destroy the city before he would ever leave it to the rebels. His urgent telegram to President Lincoln was acted upon, and General William Rosecrans arrived in time to save Nashville again. In an angry note to the president about Buell's incompetence, Johnson said, "May God save my country from some of the generals that have been conducting this war!"[2]

The danger to Nashville was still not over. For a month in 1863, the city was again under siege while Union and Confederate armies clashed nearby. Before General Rosecrans routed the rebels, the supplies of food, water, and medicines became dangerously low. And more trouble was in store for Johnson's family back in Greeneville.

The Confederates who held the town ejected Eliza Johnson and most of her family. They were forced to leave Greeneville. Their only refuge—if they could reach it—was Andrew Johnson's embattled Nashville. Eliza Johnson, her young son, her daughter Mary Stover, and Mary's three young children began the long train ride south. Upon reaching the first town, they were turned back by authorities there. Then different orders reversed that decision, and the family set off again. That pattern was repeated several times, as Eliza and her family rode through Confederate territory. At last some compassionate persons sent a message to Richmond, and the family was passed through. They were suffering from cold, hunger, and illness. It was an ordeal that would result in making Eliza, already in poor health, an invalid for the rest of her life. When the family reached Nashville, they were met by Johnson, who "wept tears of thankfulness."[3]

Nashville was now protected by a ring of Union troops under General Rosecrans.

In addition to his military troubles, Andrew Johnson suffered a family tragedy. His oldest son, Charles, thirty-three, who had joined a Union Army company, was killed when he was thrown from his horse. The news devastated the family. Eliza Johnson, it was said, never got over the loss of her son.

The Johnsons also worried about Robert, their second son. He had gotten into trouble by flaunting authority in the Union company he had joined. He was arrested, and only the efforts of his brother-in-law, Colonel Dan Stover, and other friends of his father won his release. In letters to his son, Andrew Johnson implored Robert to do his duty and to "serve his country as a sober, upright, and honorable man."[4] Shortly thereafter, while Johnson worried over the battles taking place in Tennessee, word came to him that Robert had given up his commission as a colonel in his regiment and was planning to go west. Johnson quickly averted this plan by having his son appointed to his staff as a secretary, where he could keep a close eye on the young man.

Finally, when General Grant's army in the west turned the tide against the rebels, Tennessee was cleared of Confederate forces. Now, in 1864, the end of the war was in sight. Soon, Johnson hoped, a civil government could be established in Tennessee that would lead the way for the other Confederate states. Johnson's policy was a combination of harsh treatment of the Southern rebels and generous forgiveness toward the South's actions. He called for a convention to write a new constitution for Tennessee. Ratified in February 1864, the constitution contained the provisions recommended by President Lincoln. First, readmission to the Union would be allowed when 10 percent of the registered voters signed an oath of allegiance to the Union. The second important provision was for the complete abolition of slavery according to Lincoln's Emancipation Proclamation issued on January 1, 1863.

Tennessee's acceptance of the Lincoln proposals delighted Johnson. He wired a message to the president: "Thank God for the abolition of slavery in Tennessee."[5] However, the readmission of Tennessee did not happen immediately. In fact, it did not happen until 1866. Lincoln's assassination and the fierce opposition of the Radicals in Congress wound up delaying Tennessee's admission into the Union.

The Republican party, now also called the National Union party, held its convention in Baltimore, Maryland, in June 1864. Abraham Lincoln was the candidate for reelection. Although he was the party's sole candidate, many politicians believed he would not be reelected. Lincoln himself wanted to strengthen his support by dropping his current vice-president, Hannibal Hamlin, a Radical Republican from Maine, and selecting instead a well-known Democrat in order to win some Democratic support. Such a person could bring into the party the votes of some southerners and other Unionists from the northern Democratic party. His choice for vice-president was Andrew Johnson. Lincoln wanted to show the world that not all southerners were rebels against the Union. He also wanted to reward Johnson for his loyalty to the Union cause and his courage as military governor.

Johnson heard the rumors about his name being discussed as a vice-presidential nominee, but he paid little attention. Rumors had circulated before at presidential conventions, and he regarded this particular one as merely token recognition.

However, Lincoln's choice prevailed against the Radical Republicans in Congress led by Thaddeus Stevens of Pennsylvania. When Johnson learned he had actually been nominated, he commented that the naming of a rail splitter and a tailor would certainly confound the aristocrats.[6] In accepting the honor, he predicted that under Union leadership, the government would soon quell the South's rebellion and punish the traitors for their crimes.

The Democratic party of the North nominated General George McClellan for president. In November 1864, he was defeated in an overwhelming victory for the Lincoln-Johnson ticket. Of course, none of the states that had seceded voted, as they were not yet readmitted to the Union.

James G. Blaine, a Republican congressman who would himself be running for president in 1876, said that the choice of Andrew Johnson "tended to nationalize the Republican party and thus give it great popularity throughout the nation."[7]

Johnson stayed in Nashville for the rest of the year,

hoping to leave when the state was in a more settled condition. His family was able to return to Greeneville and to their homestead, which had been well battered during the Confederate occupation.

Early in 1865, Johnson was tired, weary, and ill. For weeks, he was laid low from the effects of typhoid fever and malaria, illnesses common in the armies of both sides during the Civil War. As the time drew near for his vice-presidential inauguration, he realized that he could not in good health make the journey from Nashville to Washington. He sent a message to President Lincoln,

SOURCE DOCUMENT

"Take it quietly UNCLE ABE and I will draw it closer than ever".

"A few more stitches ANDY and the good old UNION will be mended".

THE "RAIL SPLITTER" AT WORK REPAIRING THE UNION.

In this political cartoon, Lincoln, a former rail splitter, raises the world via rail; while Johnson, a former tailor, mends the globe.

An election ticket used in the voting of 1864.

asking permission to take the oath in Nashville. Lincoln replied that he wanted Johnson by his side at the inauguration, and that it would be dangerous for him not to be there. So Johnson made the trip. Tired and sick, he arrived at the Kirkwood House hotel in the nation's capital, where he remained indoors until March 4.

It had been pouring for several days, and the inauguration ceremony had to be held in the Senate chamber. After he was sworn in, and before his acceptance speech, Johnson felt faint. He asked an aide if he could have some whiskey and was given a flask. Apparently, he took too much, and when it was time for his speech, he began in a rambling, incoherent way. Soon he was shouting and speaking wildly, referring to himself as a plebeian and jeering at the aristocrats. The audience was shocked. Many lowered their heads or averted their eyes. One biographer called Johnson's speech, "wretched stump oratory."[8] It was an embarrassing performance, and it seemed obvious to everyone that he was drunk.

After his speech ended, Johnson was taken in hand by good friends, the Blair family, and brought to their home to recover. Johnson's conduct on inauguration day was the talk of Washington for weeks. Johnson was referred to as "Andy the sot" and by the *New York World* as "this insolent, clownish creature."[9] People refused to believe that medical problems were responsible for his behavior, but President Lincoln defended his new vice-president. Once, when a senator referred to the disgraceful incident, the president said, "Don't you bother about Andy Johnson's drinking. He made a bad slip the other day, but I have known Andy Johnson for many years, and he ain't no drunkard."[10]

The war was winding down. In early April, Richmond fell to the Union Army, and Jefferson Davis fled for his life. He was soon captured and imprisoned. Lincoln invited Johnson to accompany him on a visit to the ruined Confederate capital. The good news for the people in Washington and the North was that the war was really over. It was finally made official on April 9, 1865, by the surrender at Appomattox Court House of General Robert E. Lee, the Confederate leader, to General Ulysses S. Grant. Only five days later, Abraham Lincoln was assassinated in Ford's Theatre. All jubilation over the end of the war was shattered.

In this poisoned atmosphere, Andrew Johnson became president of the United States.

8

PRESIDENT OF THE UNITED STATES

On the day Lincoln died and Andrew Johnson became president, a steady downpour drenched the city of Washington. Church bells tolled all day. The dismal weather seemed a fitting backdrop for the scene of national mourning. Assassination—the first for any president of the United States—was a shock to the entire nation.

Andrew Johnson was sworn in as president by Chief Justice Salmon P. Chase just a few hours after the official time of Lincoln's death, 7:22 A.M. on April 15, 1865. The brief ceremony that took place in the parlor of the Kirkwood House hotel was held in the presence of Lincoln's Cabinet members. Johnson assured them that he wished to carry out Abraham Lincoln's policies and requested that all the Cabinet members continue in office. They all agreed to do so. Johnson's attitude was dignified and calm, and he spoke of "free government for free people."

Mrs. Lincoln, at Johnson's invitation, remained in the White House for several weeks after her husband's death. Johnson held office in the Treasury building, in a room next to that of the secretary of the treasury, Hugh McCulloch. On April 19, there was a formal memorial funeral service held for Abraham Lincoln in the East Room of the White House. It was attended by six hundred of the government's foremost officials—justices, senators, congressmen, generals, and other notables. After the service, the assassinated president's body, laid out in a flag-draped coffin, was placed on a train, which traveled slowly to Springfield, Illinois, for burial in his home state. Silent crowds turned out all along the way to say good-bye to their slain leader and stood at respectful attention.

The first reaction to Johnson's sudden spotlight was approval. Most members of Congress and the newspaper editorials praised him. He promised to keep Lincoln's humane policies toward the South. However, the Republicans in Congress, especially those called Radicals, were opposed to Johnson's leniency toward the South. They were gratified to hear Johnson say, "Treason is a *crime*; and *crime* must be punished."[1] The Radicals thought he was speaking about all southerners, but Johnson meant only the leaders of the Confederacy, "the wealthy men who [dragged] the people into

The Lincoln funeral procession proceeds down Pennsylvania Avenue in Washington, D.C., in 1865.

secession."[2] These leaders were the real criminals, in Johnson's opinion.

In the early days after taking office, Johnson even said he would like to hang Jefferson Davis, who, after fleeing from Richmond, had been captured and imprisoned. All of Johnson's opinions were approved by the Radical Republicans, one of whom, Senator Ben Wade, declared, "Johnson, we have faith in you. There will be no trouble now in running the government."[3]

Congressman Benjamin Butler, who later became one of Johnson's fiercest enemies, pointed out that the president listened to all who came to him with advice, and that he replied to all with the same phrase: Treason must be punished. Senator Charles Sumner of Massachusetts, an ardent abolitionist, came to the president with his advice. He insisted that the only way out of the current government crisis was to free the slaves at once, unconditionally, and give them the vote. Lincoln's Emancipation Proclamation, issued on January 1, 1863, had been ignored by the rebel states for whom it was meant. Johnson listened. He said nothing, but Sumner was satisfied because the president listened to him with great attention.

Johnson was described by his visitors as "dignified, urbane and self-possessed, a most presentable person."[4] People seemed willing to forget his unfortunate inauguration day speech. According to Secretary McCulloch, whose office was next to Johnson's, there was never the slightest trace of whiskey about the president. In fact, no visitor ever saw him under the influence of liquor. Although he often drank socially, he was not an alcoholic. He worked all day in his office, dealing with piles of letters and hordes of visitors, stopping only for a meager lunch of tea and crackers.

Johnson listened to all of his advisers, but he kept his own counsel and gave no sign of accepting others' opinions. Many of his advisers misread his customary silence as acceptance of their opinions, which was hardly ever the case. Johnson would bide his time and make up his own mind.

As time went on, he continued to receive reports from trusted scouts he had sent to the South. He learned of the widespread conditions there that aroused his pity and compassion. The devastation of the countryside and the destruction of cities, the hardships of the people who were enduring life without work, food, or shelter affected his policies. He decided to reconstruct the South according to his own plans. He was certain they would have been Lincoln's, too. Then he issued two proclamations that would start the recovery process.

First, he offered a pardon to all who had participated in the rebellion. He also offered to restore all rights of property (excluding the slaves who were now free according to Lincoln's Emancipation Proclamation).

This drawing depicts the first Cabinet meeting held during Johnson's administration.

The only conditions required of the former rebel Confederates were to take an oath to support and defend the Constitution and the Union, and to abide by the Thirteenth Amendment to the Constitution, which abolished slavery. Johnson made sure to single out and refuse this general pardon to high officials and military officers of the Confederacy, governors of the seceded states, and wealthy people who owned property worth more than twenty thousand dollars. If these people desired pardons, they would have to apply in person directly to the president.

The second proclamation was to set up the political machinery necessary to return the seceded states to the Union. Under Johnson's policy, temporary governors were appointed for the southern states, the courts and post offices were restored, and elections would be called for congressmen and senators. Each state would also have a convention whose purpose would be to ratify the Thirteenth Amendment abolishing slavery. Voting rights for former slaves would be left up to the individual states to regulate.

These proclamations were the first steps taken to reestablish the Union as it had been before the Civil War, with the clear exception that slavery was now abolished. Johnson's plans were accepted by the former rebel states, and the country at large approved. There were no harsh penalties demanded, no retribution, no revenge. The spirit of Lincoln's wishes seemed to prevail, and Johnson was encouraged by the progress that had been begun to restore the South. He even relaxed the harsh treatment of Jefferson Davis and allowed Mrs. Davis to visit her imprisoned husband. (Eventually, Jefferson Davis was pardoned.)

As a result of his pardon policy, the president was swamped with visits from former Confederate officials.

SOURCE DOCUMENT

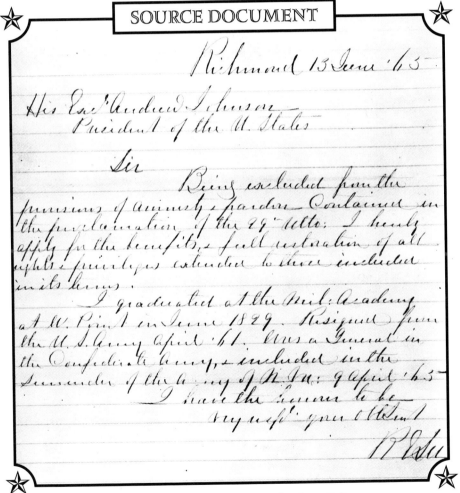

In this letter, dated June 13, 1865, General Robert E. Lee requests a pardon from President Johnson.

Congress was not in session at the time. Most of the petitioners were granted pardons after they swore allegiance to the Union. In addition, as long as he was in the White House, Johnson opened the doors to the public every afternoon at three o'clock. This procedure meant more petitions, more complaints, and more problems to be settled. For weeks, Johnson's days were pressured and hectic, and the lines waiting to see him never ended. Finally, his health broke down, and he lay in bed, gravely ill.

His older daughter, Martha Patterson, came to be with him. When her father recovered, Martha renovated the White House from its former dingy, neglected state. In August of his first summer in office, Johnson's entire family came to the White House to live with him. Eliza Johnson, now practically an invalid, could no longer act as the president's hostess. She kept to her room on the second floor.

The Johnsons' capable daughters, Martha Patterson and Mary Stover, alternated as hostess for the necessary social affairs, and both women won praise for their beauty and gracious manners. Martha expressed the family's modest attitude when she said, "We are plain people from the mountains of Tennessee, called here for a short time; I trust too much will not be expected of us."[5] Johnson's grandchildren, five in all, lightened the president's days, and he slowly began to regain his former vigorous health. He especially enjoyed driving the children and his own young son, Andrew, Jr., in his

Eliza McCardle Johnson suffered from tuberculosis and general poor health. She is pictured here later in life.

carriage to Rock Creek Park outside the city. Robert, his older son, now in his thirties, had become more responsible. He worked as an aide to his father, and took notes as the president listened to the long parade of petitioners.

Life in the White House, despite Eliza's poor health, became pleasant and restful again. The nightmares of wartime separation and hardships began to recede.

The Johnson reconstruction of the South was going well, and the public seemed to accept it. However, the Radical Republicans were furious. All of the reconstruction policies had been set while they were in recess from Congress. Johnson's policies on reconstruction were too lenient for them. They were against general pardons and forgiveness to former rebels. Above all, the Radical Republicans wanted immediate suffrage, or voting rights, to be granted to the freed slaves. Johnson considered determining the voting rights of the former slaves up to each individual state, not the job of the federal government.

Thaddeus Stevens from Pennsylvania, Speaker of the House of Representatives and one of the most radical Republicans in Congress, was old and ill, but still ready for a fight. He declared that "If something is not done to arrest the insane course of the president, he will be declared king before Congress meets."[6] Stevens and his followers got together and began to plan how to fight Johnson's reconstruction program when Congress reconvened in December 1865.

Mary Johnson Stover, Johnson's second daughter, often acted as the president's hostess in the White House, as did her sister, Martha.

Stevens called on the president and told him that unless he changed his policy toward reconstruction of the South, the party would not support him. The Speaker received no answer from Johnson. Determined to beat Johnson, Stevens then began to organize the Radical Republicans who were his supporters. First, they formed a joint committee of fifteen members from both the House of Representatives and the Senate. Called the Committee on Reconstruction, this body shifted policy making on matters regarding the South from the president to this powerful committee of Republican party leaders. Congress soon adopted the committee's first resolution—to exclude from Congress all elected representatives from the former Confederate states. Other measures revoking Johnson's reconstruction plans followed and were enforced. Suffrage for freed slaves was an important part of the Radical committee's agenda.

Johnson protested the Radicals' overturning of his plans for reconstruction of the South. In his view, the war was now past history, and despite its high toll, the Union had been preserved. The real problem now, he claimed, was to bring the former rebel states back into the Union. In reality, he maintained, the southern states had never really left the Union, because the Constitution forbade the concept of secession. Treating the seceded states as conquered subjects under military rule, as the Radicals proposed in their plan, would only cause continued hostility.

Thaddeus Stevens scoffed at Johnson's ideas. He called Johnson's plan to restore the South "a practical surrender to the Confederacy."[7] Above all, Stevens insisted, Johnson's plan made no provisions for granting the vote to the former slaves. The Radical Republicans were determined to enforce that point immediately. Johnson believed that acting too rapidly on the issue of the vote for former slaves would not be well advised. He felt that "Great changes would be dangerous to the safety of governments."[8]

The Stevens group wanted to punish the South and to insure the rights of the freed slaves. They worked

Radical Republican Thaddeus Stevens from Pennsylvania speaks out against Johnson in the House of Representatives.

tirelessly to win enough votes to defeat Johnson. The Freedmen's Bureau Act would help do both by providing education, jobs, and land for the former slaves, while keeping the southern states under military rule. Johnson vetoed the Freedmen's Bureau bill as he did all the Radicals' bills for congressional-approved reconstruction. At first, the Radicals could not muster the two-thirds vote in each house of Congress necessary to override Johnson's veto. However, by February 1866, Congress had won the necessary two-thirds vote. Still, before trying to defeat the president again, the Radicals made him an offer. If you do not veto the Freedmen's bill, they proposed, we will allow the state-elected Tennessee senators and congressmen to be readmitted to Congress. Johnson turned down that offer, explaining to his Cabinet that he "would not do wrong to secure right."[9] Although some of his Cabinet members advised him to go along, he vetoed the Freedmen's Bureau Act again. This time, the Radicals had the votes necessary to override the veto, and the act became law. Johnson explained that he "favored the admission of the freedmen to various rights, [but he intended to] encourage the South to do the right thing by itself."[10] States' rights, he kept insisting, should be upheld.

Some southern states decided to limit the advantages the Freedmen's Bureau Act gave the former slaves. On their own, these states enacted the Black Codes, which restricted the freedmen's rights and protected whites. Later, the rise of the Ku Klux Klan, a group of militant whites in the South, further intimidated African Americans and antagonized the North.

After the Radicals passed their own Reconstruction Acts in February 1866, Johnson made a rousing speech against them from the White House portico. At first, the crowd gathered below was friendly. But as Johnson became more excited, calling his enemies by name and accusing them of trying to overthrow the Constitution and the government, the mood turned ugly. Some individuals in the crowd began to heckle the president, and he responded by shouting back at them. His Cabinet members had warned him not to speak, knowing Johnson's stump-style oratory would not be appropriate for the White House. The speech was ridiculed by the Radicals and criticized by the newspapers. Nevertheless, Johnson's Cabinet supported him, although they were aware of the damage to his reputation.

Finally, Johnson decided he would go directly to the people with his case against the Radical Republicans. The congressional elections in November 1866 would be crucial in electing or rejecting his opponents. He started his campaign well, "swinging round the circle," as he put it, traveling by train through the middle and border states. By the time of his return trip, however, the Radicals had gathered their forces against him. When Johnson campaigned, he was often met by hecklers who had been planted in the audience to counter him with strong opposition. As he tried to speak, the crowds became unruly. He reacted by becoming angry and shouting back at the hecklers. Eventually, he lost much support.

The November elections gave the Radicals a victory in Congress. The president's image was badly damaged, and "Andyjohnsonism," as his enemies called his cause, was turned down. Under their own Reconstruction Acts, the Radicals were able to pass many more bills through Congress, especially those guaranteeing the civil rights of African Americans. Johnson considered these bills unconstitutional because they made citizenship a federal matter rather than a right for each individual state to decide. He was vetoing most of the bills sent to him, and his vetoes were being regularly overridden. Many northerners who were not especially radical supported Congress. Spokesmen for the former slaves, like Horace Greeley, the newspaper editor, and Henry Ward Beecher, a popular clergyman, strongly upheld Congress's push for African-American rights.

The Reconstruction Acts passed by Congress over Johnson's vetoes crippled the president's power. The only powers that remained to him were the right to grant pardons and the use of patronage, or the ability to appoint people to political jobs without requiring the approval of the Senate. In 1867, Johnson removed more than a thousand postmasters and replaced them with his own choices.

The tension and ill will between the Radicals and Johnson increased. Now there was talk of impeachment. The subject was being seriously considered by his enemies. Impeachment meant being accused of "high crimes and misdemeanors" as stated in the Constitution. Accusing a president of these crimes would have to come from the House of Representatives in a formal statement. To be convicted of the crimes, the president would first need to be tried in court in a trial held in the Senate. The accused would be removed from office only if he was found guilty of the crimes by a two-thirds majority vote of the Senate.

For a while, because there were still some conservative or moderate Republicans in Congress, as well as a few northern Democrats, the impeachment process was held up. Until the Radicals had a firm two-thirds majority in the Senate, they would bide their time.

In March 1867, the Radicals believed they had found a way to bring a definite "crime" against Johnson. He not only vetoed the Tenure of Office Act, which Congress had submitted, but he was likely to disobey it as unconstitutional if Congress passed it, overriding his veto. The Tenure of Office Act would prevent the president from dismissing any government official, even any of his own Cabinet members, who had been appointed with Senate consent. It was well known that Johnson's secretary of war, Edwin Stanton, was a spy within the Cabinet. He was working for the Radical congressmen against the president. It was also known that Johnson would like to fire Stanton. Now, the stage was set for the confrontation Congress had arranged.

9

IMPEACHMENT AND TRIAL

When the Tenure of Office Act passed Congress in March 1867 after its veto by President Johnson, the Radicals scornfully declared "King Andy is dead."[1] Under the leadership of Thaddeus Stevens and Ben Wade, Congress had been working for some time to assure a two-thirds Republican majority in both houses. They had hurried along Nebraska's admission to the Union as the thirty-seventh state, hoping to get two more Republican senators after Nebraska was admitted. Now they took up the cause of admitting Colorado as a state because they knew that territory was radical in its politics and could be counted on for two more anti-Johnson senators. Johnson quickly vetoed the bill calling for Colorado's admission, claiming it was a "farce of pretending that Colorado was ready to become a state."[2] The Radicals lost their attempt to admit Colorado. With only twenty-seven thousand in population, far less than what was required, the territory had to postpone its statehood for several years.

However, the Radicals succeeded in eliminating two conservative nominees proposed by the president to be Supreme Court justices. The Radicals managed to eliminate them by persuading Congress to pass a bill that gave it the power to reduce the number of justices.[3] That act was overturned in 1869, when the number of justices was set permanently at nine.

Thaddeus Stevens's skill in driving Congress his way had to be admitted, even admired, by many. As old and sick as he was, Stevens's maneuvering was brilliant. He was called "a master of parliamentary tricks."[4]

By now, Johnson had become used to congressional opposition, insults, and false rumors. There had even been one accusing him of being part of the conspiracy to murder President Lincoln. But Johnson considered the Tenure of Office Act the most outrageous of all the Radicals' plans. Certainly, it was unconstitutional. Just as the Radicals in Congress had expected and hoped, the president decided to test the Tenure of Office Act.

In August 1867, he dismissed Secretary Stanton from the War Office and appointed General Ulysses S. Grant, the great Civil War hero, in Stanton's place. Because of Grant's popularity with the public and the members of Congress, nothing was done by Congress for a few months to challenge this appointment. Finally, in March 1868, the Senate passed a resolution stating that the president lacked the power to remove Stanton from office and appoint a replacement. The Senate cited the Tenure of Office Act, which it claimed Johnson had purposely ignored, as authority for its resolution.

A note was sent to General Grant by Congress warning him of possible trouble, and he immediately left the War Office. To make matters worse, Grant handed the keys to the office back to former Secretary Stanton, who promptly returned to his former workplace. Enraged, Johnson called on General Grant to appear before him and the rest of his Cabinet to explain his action. Except for Stanton, who refused to leave the War Office, all of the Cabinet members supported President Johnson. Grant could not give a satisfactory excuse for his behavior, but it was known that he had his own presidential ambitions and was looking forward to the election in 1868. He could not afford to go against the wishes of Congress. He would need its support.

Johnson insisted he had a constitutional right to remove Stanton from office, so he ordered General Lorenzo Thomas to take over the War Office. The president notified Congress that even if his own removal was sure to follow Stanton's dismissal, he would not hesitate to carry out his constitutional right to select his own Cabinet. General Thomas proved weak in dealing with Stanton and soon left him still sitting in the War Office.

Secretary of War Edwin Stanton was fired by Johnson, but he refused to leave the War Office. The president's attempt to remove Stanton from his Cabinet position was the main evidence used to impeach Johnson.

Encouraged by Thaddeus Stevens and Senator Charles Sumner who told Stanton to "stick,"[5] Stanton sat on.

The Reconstruction Committee of the Joint Houses of Congress, through its spokesman Thaddeus Stevens, then called for a vote to impeach the president, or formally charge or accuse him of "high crimes and misdemeanors in office."[6] The president's removal of Stanton from his Cabinet position was the main evidence against Johnson. The vote in the House of Representatives calling for impeachment was 126 to 47 against it. The Democrats, numbering only eleven representatives, voted no.

Ben Wade, president *pro tem* of the Senate (the most senior of the majority party), was pleased about the impeachment declaration. He would be next in line for the presidency, since there was no vice-president, if Johnson, after being tried, was found guilty and forced to leave office. Wade boasted that he would be sitting in the president's chair in ten days. Congressman Ben Butler, commonly called "the beast," gave a three-hour speech in the House of Representatives in which he ridiculed Johnson.

Secretary of the Navy Welles, one of the president's most loyal friends, wrote that "the Constitution breakers were trying [to destroy] the Constitution defender."[7]

Everything had been prepared by the Radicals for Johnson's impeachment trial. Eleven charges were listed, but as everyone knew, only the eleventh charge, the one related to Stanton's removal, really counted.

SOURCE DOCUMENT

THE PAROQUET OF THE WH—E HO—E.

This political cartoon portrays Johnson as a parrot repeating the word Constitution. It refers to his constant reliance on the Constitution to support and interpret his political positions.

A board of seven managers, including five Radical congressmen, was elected to prepare the impeachment case in the House of Representatives. The Senate, acting as the High Court of Impeachment, would be the jury, presided over by Chief Justice Salmon Chase.

On March 13, 1868, notice was served on the president that the impeachment trial was ready to begin, and that he was expected to make a formal appearance the next day. The following day, the sergeant-at-arms in the Senate announced in a loud voice, "Andrew Johnson, President of the United States, appear and answer the

The board of seven managers elected to prepare the impeachment case against Johnson in the House of Representatives. Seated, left to right: Benjamin Butler (Mass.); Thaddeus Stevens and Thomas Williams (Penn.); John Bingham (Ohio). Standing left to right: James Wilson (Iowa); George Boutwell (Mass.); John Logan (Ill.).

Articles of Impeachment exhibited against you by the House of Representatives of the United States."[8] The Radicals expected to see the president appear in person. However, they were disappointed. Johnson did not appear, having decided that he would instead be represented by counsel. After a short delay, his lawyers appeared and asked for time to prepare their defense— forty days to be exact—but they were given only ten. Henry Stanbery, who had been the attorney general, resigned his position in order to defend Johnson. He was outraged. This case, he said, was "of the greatest magnitude we have ever had, [and] is to be treated [by the managers] as if it were a case before a police court."[9]

Stanbery obtained one of the best-known lawyers in the country, Benjamin R. Curtis of Boston, to lead the defense team, which included an old friend of Johnson's from Greeneville, Judge Thomas Nelson. None of Johnson's lawyers would accept fees, maintaining that their work was given as a public service.

The defense lawyers worked day and night to respond to the charges within the allotted ten days. The president contributed a great deal to his own case. Curtis, the Boston lawyer, was greatly impressed by the president's sincerity and honesty. "He firmly believes he is right," the lawyer said. "True in his devotion to the Constitution . . . his ideas are right and true . . . firm as a rock."[10]

There were strong emotions and convictions on both sides expressed throughout the country. The chairman of the Republican party sent a telegram to party leaders in all the states, declaring that if the impeachment trial of Johnson failed to convict, there would be "great danger to the peace of the country."[11]

The Radicals in Congress meant to leave nothing to chance. They made fiery speeches against Andrew Johnson. They held meetings in their own homes to devise new ways of putting pressure on the senators. They even asked other members of the House of Representatives to write letters and send telegrams denouncing Johnson to their constituents back home.

All of this activity came from elected officials whose impeachment oath bound them to do impartial justice.[12]

However, President Johnson was not without support from a great deal of the public. Many heartening messages came to him—scores of letters and several newspaper editorials. He was assured of sympathy and approval from many sources. "For the sake of God and liberty, stand firm," one said. Others told him, "If you want troops, let us know . . . [we are] anxious to rally to your support."[13] Of course, Johnson ignored any talk of violence. He felt he could endure the trial. Even if he were convicted, he said, "he would care nothing . . . if he stood acquitted by the people."[14]

The Radicals continued to spread their accusations far and wide. Johnson was denounced, scorned, and ridiculed. Just in case slander did not work, his enemies tried using threats and bribery. Offers were made to corrupt Johnson's defenders. Secretary of State Seward, Johnson's able ally, was assured by a spokesman for Ben

Wade that he would be retained in his Cabinet post if he did nothing to interfere with the impeachment process. Ben Wade expected to be president as soon as Johnson was removed from office. "I will see you damned first,"[15] was Seward's reply to the offer.

The trial finally began on March 13, 1868. Special tickets were printed for admission to the Senate galleries. From there, the public, those lucky enough to obtain the sought-after tickets, could witness the great event, which would last until May 16.

The seven managers from the House presented the evidence and questioned witnesses. Spectators at the trial noted that the managers were no match for Johnson's skillful defense lawyers. After a few days of

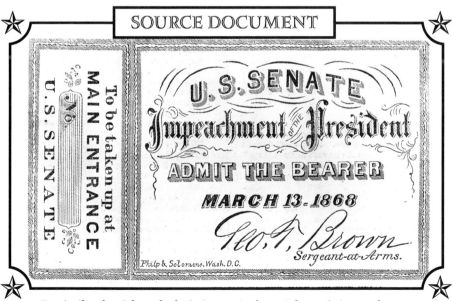

SOURCE DOCUMENT

Facsimile of a ticket of admission to Andrew Johnson's impeachment trial, which began on March 13, 1868.

This later portrait of Johnson, probably taken around 1868, shows the strains of his ordeal in office.

attention to the eleven articles of impeachment, the accusers realized that the only relevant count against Johnson was the dismissal of Secretary of War Stanton. So it was decided to present that article first.

The Senate, fifty-four members strong, would be the jury. They would decide the verdict after the trial presentations. Of the senators, nine were Democrats and three were called "Johnson conservatives," or Republicans who favored the president. That meant there were twelve men in all whose votes would be prejudiced to acquit the president, or dismiss the charges against him. The Radical Republicans would need thirty-six votes, or two thirds of the Senate, to arrive at a guilty verdict. That meant they could still succeed in removing the president from office if no more than eighteen senators supported him. The Radicals were confident of winning those thirty-six votes, although there were a few senators whose views were not publically known.

Before the trial began, bribes, threats, and intense pressure were used by the anti-Johnson side to harass the small group of senators thought to be undecided. One fearless senator, William Fessenden of Maine, stood up early to the Radicals and said he would vote to acquit the president. The remaining "undecided" six senators who had not revealed how they were going to vote were strongly urged to go with the majority. They were warned they would be called traitors to their party if they voted for acquittal. They were also threatened with the loss of their Senate seats in the next election.

This drawing, which appeared in Harper's Weekly, *shows the impeachment trial of Johnson in the Senate chamber.*

Senator John Henderson of Missouri was young and engaged to be married. He worried about the effect the loss of his job might have on his fiancée. Senator Lyman Trumbull of Louisiana, the author of the Freedmen's Bureau Bill, was threatened with death if he failed to convict. Senator Joseph Fowler of Tennessee was told he would be accused of committing treason to his governor if he did not vote against Johnson. Senator Peter Van Winkle of West Virginia would be accused of treason to his party, and so would Senator Edmund Ross of Kansas who would be going against his state's direction if he failed to vote for conviction. Senator James Grimes of Iowa, known to be a friend of Johnson's, was so upset by the Radicals' pressure, it was claimed, that he was stricken with paralysis and was not expected to appear at the trial.

For almost two months after the trial began, the Radicals did their best to destroy the president. They did not hesitate to present false witnesses, questionable evidence, and slanderous name-calling. In one speech Ben Butler called Johnson "a murderer and a robber of the treasury."[16]

During this time, the president stayed in the White House, doing his work. An aide who attended all of the Senate proceedings reported to him every evening. Several times, Johnson longed to go to the Senate chamber and defend himself, but his lawyers wisely discouraged him.

At last the trial ended.

The tension in the Senate chamber was as thick as a cloud on May 16, as the senators withdrew to consider their verdict. Then they returned for the roll call. Just as it was about to begin, a totally unexpected sight caused a ripple of excitement. Senator Grimes, still paralyzed, was carried in from his sick bed to his Senate chair. He would vote after all. The roll call began. Thirty-five senators replied "guilty" as their names were called. The seven who had been undecided, or unwilling to commit themselves, were called last. With just one more guilty vote, Johnson's presidency would be ended.

As expected, Senator Fessenden returned a "not guilty" judgment. Then there were six senators left. Radicals strained to hear just one more "guilty" vote. Senators Grimes, Henderson, Trumbull, Fowler, and Van Winkle were called. The excitement rose as each, in

SOURCE DOCUMENT

Fortieth Congress U.S. Second Session

SENATE CHAMBER.

MAY 16TH AND 26TH 1868.

The vote of the Senate, sitting as a High Court of Impeachment for the trial of **ANDREW JOHNSON**, President of the United States, upon the 11th, 2nd and 3rd Articles.

S.P. Chase, Chief Justice.   *J.W. Forney,* Secretary.

Guilty.

1. *[illegible]*
2. *H.W. Corbett*
3. *Cornelius Cole*
4. *A.M. Flora*
5. *Wm M Stewart*
6. *J.W. Patterson*
7. *Justin S. Morrill*
8. *James W. Nye*
9. *Timothy Howe*
10. *Henry Wilson*
11. *A.H. Cragin*
12. *[illegible]*
13. *Jas Harlan*
14. *O.S. Ferry*
15. *Aly. Ramsey*
16. *John Conness*
17. *Geo.F. Edmunds*
18. *Fred T. Frelinghuysen*
19. *H.B. Anthony*
20. *Jm. Howard*
21. *S.C. Pomeroy*
22. *W.J. Willey*
23. *Rich. Yates*
24. *Charles Sumner*
25. *Aaron H. Cragin*
26. *Geo.H. Williams*
27. *Zz. Chandler*
28. *E.D. Morgan*
29. *John Sherman*
30. *John M. Thayer*
31. *Roscoe Conkling*
32. *C.S. Drake*
33. *Simon Cameron*
34. *T.W. Tipton*
35. *O.P. Morton*

Not Guilty.

1. *T.A. Hendricks*
2. *A.G. Buckalew*
3. *Trinton*
4. *J.R. Doolittle*
5. *Thos. C. McCreery*
6. *George Vickers*
7. *J.B. Henderson*
8. *Lyman Trumbull*
9. *E.G. Ross*
10. *W.P. Fessenden*
11. *Garrett Davis*
12. *J.A. Bayard*
13. *Jos. S. Fowler*
14. *Jos Grimes*
15. *Daniel S. Norton*
16. *Willard Saulsbury*
17. *Reverdy Johnson*
18. *P.G. Van Winkle*
19. *James Dixon*

Entered according to Act of Congress in the year 1868, by JAMES H. M°BRIDE of Mansfield, Ohio, in the Clerk's Office of the District Court of the District of Columbia.

Signatures of the voters for and against impeachment of the president.

turn, declared the president "not guilty." Senator Ross was the last to be called. His vote would determine the outcome. Every voice, every sound was stilled. In the hushed Senate, with the Radicals' faces glowering, Ross stood and stated in a firm, clear voice, "not guilty." Andrew Johnson was acquitted.

The room exploded. Young William Crook, Johnson's bodyguard, who was sitting in the gallery, jumped to his feet, tore down the stairs, and ran all the way to the White House. On his way out, he had seen Thaddeus Stevens being held up on the shoulders of two attendants. "His face was black with rage," Crook noted, "[and he] was waving his arms and shouting, 'The country is going to the devil!'"[17]

When Crook arrived at the White House, he saw a group gathered around the president. Included were Johnson's attorneys Stanbery and Nelson, who, as soon as the verdict had been announced, burst forth from the Senate into a waiting carriage outside and raced to the White House. Crook saw that the president already knew he had won so he ran upstairs to Eliza Johnson's room and told her the good news, "He is acquitted!" She rose from her chair and grasped his hand. "Crook, I knew he'd be acquitted; I knew it,"[18] she said.

Soon there was a great procession of wellwishers calling on the president. He was described as "dignified and restraint [sic], without arrogance or an appearance of unseemly joy."[19]

10
AFTERMATH

After Andrew Johnson was acquitted of the "crimes" he was tried for, the Radicals turned their abuse on the seven Republicans who had voted to acquit him. All seven were accused of treason to their party. Some newspapers like the *Chicago Tribune*, directed by Horace Greeley, called them "corrupt and shameless scoundrels."[1]

Senator Edmund Ross from Kansas, in particular, was the object of the Radicals' rage because he had ignored every means at their disposal to bully and intimidate him. They had expected Ross to yield to their pressure tactics. Now they would show this "skunk and perjurer"[2] what it meant to oppose them. The Radicals could not force his resignation from the Senate, but they could do their utmost to keep him from being reelected by the voters back home. They succeeded in this goal, and Ross lost reelection when the time came.

In order to earn a living, he opened a printing shop in the town of Coffeyville, Kansas. One day a huge thug entered the shop and beat Ross unmercifully. The former senator never fully recovered from that attack. To make matters worse, a tornado struck the town and destroyed his printing shop. Not until many years later, when Grover Cleveland was president, did Ross's luck change. Cleveland appointed him governor of the territory of New Mexico, and in 1907, Congress voted Ross a pension for the service he had performed as a Union soldier in the Civil War.

Four other senators who had voted not guilty, Fowler, Van Winkle, Trumbull, and Henderson, were similarly targets of the Radicals' revenge. All were denied reelection and were forced to return to private life. Senator Fessenden of Maine died in 1869, before his reelection could be lost, as would surely have happened if he had lived. Senator Grimes of Iowa who had so dramatically left his sick bed to cast his decisive vote, never fully recovered his health. Soon after the trial, he resigned from the Senate.

Only one man who had defied the Radicals, Senator Henderson of Missouri, who also lost his campaign for reelection, lived long enough to win the respect of the Republican party. After a successful career practicing law and helping to organize the moderate Republicans, he became the permanent chairman at the Republican party convention in 1884. There, so many years after the impeachment trial, Senator Charles Sumner of Massachusetts, who had spoken and voted against Johnson in 1868, confessed to Henderson that he had been wrong.

But to Andrew Johnson, the outcome of the trial was victory enough. Congratulations poured in from all over the country. On the day after the trial ended, guns were fired in many cities in honor of the verdict. Twilight processions were held. Even the city of Lancaster, Pennsylvania, Thaddeus Stevens's hometown, sent congratulations to the president, telling him "Justice has triumphed over party."[3]

Edwin Stanton left the War Office, which he had so stubbornly held onto throughout the controversy, as soon as the verdict was announced. He sent a message of his withdrawal to Johnson, who refused to recognize him by a reply. Johnson then temporarily appointed Secretary of State Seward to the position until the Senate later confirmed his choice of General John Schofield as secretary of war.

In June 1868, Johnson sent out a Proclamation of General Amnesty granting unconditional pardons to everyone in the Confederate states except those people already under indictment. The proclamation included the release from prison of former Confederate president Jefferson Davis. Not surprisingly, the Democratic party ignored Andrew Johnson's unlikely bid for the 1868 presidential nomination. The party chose the former

The Radical Republicans later retaliated against Senator Edmund Ross of Kansas, shown above, who delivered the final "not guilty" vote, acquitting Johnson of the impeachment charges against him.

governor of New York state, Horatio Seymour. However, in the election he lost to the Republican party candidate, General Ulysses S. Grant.

After the impeachment trial, President Johnson and his family enjoyed some peaceful months in the White House. They did more entertaining. On the president's sixtieth birthday, December 29, 1868, they held a large children's party in the White House, which had been transformed into a fairyland. The president's two daughters stood on the receiving line to welcome the hordes of visitors. Their children took part in dancing, along with a group from a dancing academy. Eliza Johnson made a rare public appearance.

On New Year's Day, there was another grand reception, jammed with people who turned out in great numbers, as had been customary in Andrew Jackson's day. Ben Butler, Johnson's former Radical enemy came, and the president shook his hand. Ulysses S. Grant, the president-elect, was not present.

Finally, on Washington's birthday, another reception closed the social entertaining season of the Johnson administration.

The Radicals in Congress were still sore. They eventually repealed the Tenure of Office Act, but rejected all of Johnson's nominees for ambassador posts. The Fifteenth Amendment was passed with Radical backing. It reinforced the former slaves' right to vote, which was guaranteed in the Thirteenth and

Fourteenth additions to the Constitution, called the Reconstruction Amendments.

When the day came for Grant's inauguration as president, the ill feeling between him and Johnson was apparent. Grant had already announced that he would not ride to the inauguration, as was the tradition, in the same carriage with the outgoing president. Johnson responded that he would neither ride in the same carriage with, nor speak to Grant, the man who he believed had betrayed him. The inaugural committee, trying to compromise, suggested using two carriages. But when the day came, Johnson told his Cabinet members, who were expecting to attend the inauguration with him, that none of them would go to the ceremony at all. They would finish up their work by noon and then all leave the White House together.

Shortly after noon, Johnson shook hands with his Cabinet members. Then he drove off in his carriage to the home of Secretary Welles, where he and his family stayed for a few days. Shortly after the Cabinet members left the White House, the Grant party arrived and took over.

On the way home to Greeneville, Johnson received a friendly reception all along the way, even in towns that had once denounced him. Now his train stopped at every station, and the crowds cheered him. When the family reached Greeneville, they rode under a banner that read "Welcome home, Andrew Johnson, Patriot."

The Johnsons made their home livable again after

the years of occupation, and resumed life among their good friends and neighbors. The Johnson daughters and their respective families lived nearby, the Pattersons in Greeneville and the Stovers on a farm in Carter County.

Shortly after the Johnsons returned to Greeneville, a family tragedy occurred. Robert Johnson, at the age of thirty-five, committed suicide. The family mourned their son and brother, as well as his "wasted great opportunities"[4] due to his addiction to alcohol.

At last Andrew Johnson was free from the pressures of office and the battles with Congress. However, now he was restless. He commented that "to live he must be busy."[5] He dreaded retirement and rest. However, although he craved activity, he withdrew his name when it was put up by his friends as a candidate for the House of Representatives. It was the Senate to which he longed to return. Johnson declared, "I would rather have the vindication of my state by electing me to my old seat in the Senate of the United States than to be monarch of the grandest empire on earth."[6]

To attain his goal, he campaigned for election by the state legislature to a seat in the United States Senate whenever one became available. For several years he did not win, but Johnson's old fire brought large crowds out to hear him wherever he spoke. He was described as dignified and courtly, no longer ranting, but "his eyes were ablaze" and "his remarkable magnetism compelled people to listen to him."[7] He was still champion of the Union, the Constitution, and the common people; he was still opposed to the radical reconstruction of the South.

In 1873, an epidemic of cholera swept through east Tennessee. Johnson caught the disease and for several weeks he was at the point of death. At last he rallied, but he never recovered his former strength. However, he was still ambitious, and in 1875 he was finally elected to the United States Senate. "Thank God for the vindication,"[8] he said. It was a personal triumph. The newspapers paid tribute to his pluck, his integrity, his honesty. Going back to the Senate was considered a remarkable victory; Johnson was the only former president to be elected to the Senate.

On the first day of his return, even some of his old enemies greeted him, and flowers were piled on his desk. He made one speech before Congress adjourned for the summer. It was his last great public performance, in which he criticized the policies of President Grant as trampling the Constitution underfoot. The speech had drawn crowds to hear him and resulted in "wild applause"[9] from the spectators in the Senate galleries. Afterward, a friend who called on Johnson at his quarters in the Willard Hotel on Pennsylvania Avenue commented that his present rooms were not nearly as grand and spacious as those he had occupied further up the avenue. "No," Johnson answered the friend. "But they are more comfortable."[10]

While Congress adjourned, Johnson renewed old friendships back home. He visited his daughters and grandchildren. One day in July, he took the train from Greeneville to Mary Stover's farm in Carter County. He arrived there, but shortly afterward he was suddenly felled by a stroke. He died the next day, July 31, 1875, at age sixty-seven. He was buried in a spot on his favorite hilltop outside of Greeneville, where a monument was later erected to him. Andrew Johnson, in death, was wrapped in the flag of his country, his well-worn copy of the Constitution as his pillow—just as he had wished. His third commitment after the flag and the Constitution was to the common people, who recognized him as one of their own.

Today, Andrew Johnson's memory lives on in Greeneville, Tennessee, where his homes, tailor shop, and monument make up the Andrew Johnson National Historic Site. On the monument at his grave site, these words are engraved: "His faith in the people never wavered."

11

LEGACY

A ndrew Johnson is not likely to rate high on any historian's scale of notable presidential achievers. However, Johnson will always be remembered for his dramatic defense against ruthless enemies, his courage in facing the impeachment charges brought against him by his enemies in Congress, his honesty, and his determination to do what he considered to be right.

His reputation has "alternately suffered and flourished"[1] over the years, changing with the times. His courageous stand on behalf of the Union and the provisions of the Constitution was offset by his beliefs in white supremacy and his failure to adjust to the nation's growing industrial expansion. His outlook remained a provincial one appropriate for a nation of small farmers and mechanics. He was "a child of his time but he failed to grow with it."[2] When Johnson left office, however, he had the support and good wishes of much of the public.

During the four years of his administration, sandwiched between the more famous terms of Abraham Lincoln and Ulysses S. Grant, Johnson represented the country in the unsettling times following the Civil War. Johnson's own administration, overshadowed by the impeachment trial, could still point to some positive accomplishments. Secretary of State Seward helped the nation acquire Alaska from Russia for the bargain price of $7.2 million. Even so, some in Congress thought he paid too much. In time, "Seward's Folly," as the purchase would later be called, was appreciated for its vast natural resources as well as its strategic northern position. Seward was also responsible for acquiring Midway Island in the Pacific. A small, uninhabited island, Midway served as a naval base for the United States in World War II.

A Mexican incident was peacefully settled under Johnson's administration when the United States invoked the Monroe Doctrine of 1823. France had installed the Archduke Maximilian of Austria as its puppet ruler in an attempted occupation of Mexico. President Johnson's message to France stated the Monroe Doctrine's resolve that no foreign occupation of any country in the Western Hemisphere would be tolerated by the United States. France withdrew its occupying forces.

William Henry Seward was the secretary of state under Lincoln and Johnson and negotiator of the purchase of Alaska, which became known as "Seward's Folly."

With Secretary Seward on his side, President Johnson managed to stay out of all further foreign entanglements.

His ultimate victory over the impeachment charges brought against him and his greatest vindication came many years after his death: The Tenure of Office Act, on which Johnson's impeachment trial was based, was repealed by Congress in 1887, and the Supreme Court of the United States declared it unconstitutional in 1926.

Chronology

1808—Born in Raleigh, North Carolina, on December 29, the second son of Jacob and Mary (Polly) McDonough Johnson.

1812—Death of father, Jacob Johnson.

1822—At the age of fourteen, bound until age twenty-one as a tailor's apprentice.

1824—Ran away from Raleigh to evade possible punishment for a mischievous prank.

1824–1826 —Roamed across South Carolina and Tennessee, working his way as a tailor's helper.

1826—Returned to Raleigh and moved family to Greeneville, Tennessee, where he opened his own tailor shop.

1827—Married Eliza McCardle of Greeneville.

1828—Birth of daughter, Martha; elected to the Greeneville town council.

1830—Birth of son, Charles; elected mayor of Greeneville.

1831—Purchased larger house and moved tailor shop close to it.

1832—Birth of daughter, Mary.

1834—Birth of son, Robert.

1835—Elected to Tennessee state legislature.

1837—Defeated for reelection; began wider campaign, backed by the common people.

1839—Reelected to state legislature.

1841—Elected to state senate.

1843—Elected to United States Congress; lived part time in Washington, D.C. Reelected four times; served until 1853.

1846—Introduced Homestead Act ("Free Land for Free People") in Congress; bill defeated.

1852—Birth of third son, Andrew, Jr; wife's health declined; moved into the family's final "homestead."

1853 —Elected governor of Tennessee; reelected
–1855 for second term.

1857—Elected to United States Senate; served until 1862.

1860—Abraham Lincoln elected president; secession of southern states; beginning of Civil War.

1862—Appointed by President Lincoln to serve as military governor of Tennessee; Homestead Act passed.

1863—Death of son Charles, age thirty-three, who was thrown from a horse.

1864—Elected vice-president for Lincoln's second term.

1865—Civil War ended April 9. Became president April 15, upon the assassination of Abraham Lincoln.

1866—Made "Swing Around the Circle" to campaign for moderate congressmen.

1868—Beginning of impeachment proceedings by House of Representatives, February 24; trial from March to May; acquittal by the Senate, May 16.

1869—Completed presidential term; returned to Greeneville; suicide death of son Robert, age thirty-five.

1869
–1872 —Campaigned for election to the United States Senate; defeated several times.

1875—Elected to the United States Senate in January; served from March to July.

Died at daughter Mary's home on July 31, age sixty-seven.

Chapter Notes

Chapter 1. Black Friday
1. James E. Sefton, *Andrew Johnson and the Uses of Constitutional Power* (Boston: Little Brown and Co., 1980), p. 106.

Chapter 2. The Tailor's Apprentice
1. Hans L. Trefousse, *Andrew Johnson: A Biography* (New York: W. W. Norton and Co., 1989), p. 20.
2. Ibid., p. 21.
3. Robert W. Winston, *Andrew Jackson: Plebeian and Patriot* (New York: Barnes and Noble, reprinted edition, 1969), p. 11.
4. George Fort Milton, *The Age of Hate: Andrew Johnson and the Radicals* (Hamden, Conn.: Archon Books, 1965), p. 65.

Chapter 3. At Home in Greeneville
1. G. Allen Foster, *Impeached: The President Who Almost Lost His Job* (New York: Criterion Books, 1964), p. 32.
2. Lately Thomas, *The First President Johnson* (New York: William Morrow and Co., Inc., 1968), p. 29.

Chapter 4. Tailor Turned Politician
1. Hans L. Trefousse, *Andrew Johnson: A Biography* (New York: W. W. Norton and Co., 1989), p. 40.
2. Ibid., p. 57.
3. Ibid., p. 166.
4. Robert W. Winston, *Andrew Johnson: Plebeian and Patriot* (New York: Barnes and Noble, reprinted edition, 1969), p. 41.

Chapter 5. On the National Scene

1. Robert W. Winston, *Andrew Johnson: Plebeian and Patriot* (New York: Barnes and Noble, reprinted edition, 1969), p. 75.
2. Ibid., p. 50.
3. George Fort Milton, *The Age of Hate: Andrew Johnson and the Radicals* (Hamden, Conn.: Archon Books, 1965), p. 96.
4. Ibid., p. 97.
5. Hans L. Trefousse, *Andrew Johnson: A Biography* (New York: W.W. Norton and Co., 1989), p. 88.
6. Ibid., p. 104.
7. Zachary Kent, *Andrew Johnson: Encyclopedia of Presidents* (Chicago: Children's Press, 1989), p. 46.
8. Winston, p. 264.
9. Ibid., p. 139.
10. Winston, p. 93.

Chapter 6. Toward Civil War

1. Lately Thomas, *The First President Johnson* (New York: William Morrow and Co., Inc., 1968), p. 120.
2. *Oxford Dictionary of Quotations*, 4th ed. (New York: Oxford University Press, 1992), p. 421.
3. Hans L. Trefousse, *Andrew Johnson: A Biography* (New York: W. W. Norton and Co., 1989), p. 100.

Chapter 7. Military Governor

1. Lately Thomas, *The First President Johnson* (New York: William Morrow and Co., Inc., 1968), p. 205.
2. Ibid., p. 240.
3. Ibid., p. 243.
4. Ibid., p. 262.
5. Robert Winston, *Andrew Johnson: Plebeian and Patriot* (New York: Barnes and Noble, reprinted edition, 1969), p. 257.
6. Ibid.
7. Ibid.
8. Ibid., p. 264.

9. Zachary Kent, *Andrew Johnson: Encyclopedia of Presidents* (Chicago: Children's Press, 1989), p. 46.

10. Ibid., p. 47.

Chapter 8. President of the United States

1. Lately Thomas, *The First President Johnson* (New York: William Morrow and Co., Inc., 1968), p. 324.

2. George Fort Milton, *The Age of Hate: Andrew Johnson and the Radicals* (Hamden, Conn.: Archon Books, 1965), p. 242.

3. Thomas, p. 324.

4. Ibid., p. 328.

5. Hans L. Trefousse, *Andrew Johnson: A Biography* (New York: W. W. Norton and Co., 1989), p. 239.

6. Thomas, p. 359.

7. Ibid., p. 358.

8. Trefousse, p. 236.

9. Robert W. Winston, *Andrew Johnson: Plebeian and Patriot* (New York: Barnes and Noble, reprinted edition, 1969), p. 262.

10. James E. Sefton, *Andrew Johnson and the Uses of Constitutional Power* (Boston: Little Brown and Co., 1980), p. 129.

Chapter 9. Impeachment and Trial

1. Robert W. Winston, *Andrew Johnson: Plebeian and Patriot* (New York: Barnes and Noble, reprinted edition, 1969), p. 372.

2. Lately Thomas, *The First President Johnson* (New York: William Morrow and Inc., 1968), p. 434.

3. Hans L. Trefousse, *Andrew Johnson: A Biography* (New York: W. W. Norton and Co., 1989), p. 237.

4. Winston, p. 400.

5. Ibid., p. 420.

6. Ibid., p. 438.

7. George Fort Milton, *The Age of Hate: Andrew Johnson and the Radicals* (Hamden, Conn.: Archon Books, 1965), p. 529.

8. Ibid., p. 531.

9. Thomas, pp. 586–587.

10. Milton, p. 598.

11. Ibid., p. 584.

12. Ibid., p. 524.

13. Ibid., p. 528.

14. Ibid.

15. James E. Sefton, *Andrew Johnson and the Uses of Constitutional Power* (Boston: Little Brown and Co., 1980), p. 176.

16. Milton, p. 611.

17. Ibid.

18. Thomas, p. 607.

19. Milton, p. 612

Chapter 10. Aftermath

1. George Fort Milton, *The Age of Hate: Andrew Johnson and the Radicals* (Hamden, Conn.: Archon Books, 1965), p. 614.

2. Ibid., p. 622.

3. Ibid., p. 613.

4. Hans L. Trefousse, *Andrew Johnson: A Biography* (New York: W. W. Norton and Co., 1989), p. 356.

5. Milton, p. 648.

6. Ibid., p. 662.

7. Ibid., p. 664.

8. Trefousse, p. 372.

9. Milton, p. 672.

10. Boller, Paul F. Jr., *Presidential Anecdotes* (New York: Oxford University Press, 1981), p. 151.

Chapter 11. Legacy

1. Hans L. Trefousse, *Andrew Johnson: A Biography* (New York: W. W. Norton and Co., 1989), p. 378.

2. Ibid., p. 379.

Further Reading

Benedict, Michael Les. *The Impeachment and Trial of Andrew Johnson*. New York: W. W. Norton and Co., Inc., 1973.

Castel, Albert. *The Presidency of Andrew Johnson*. Lawrence, Kans.: The Regents Press, 1979.

Dubowski, Cathy E. *Andrew Johnson: Rebuilding the Union*. Parsippany, N.J.: Silver Burdett Press, 1990.

Foster, G. Allen. *Impeached: The President Who Almost Lost His Job*. New York: Criterion Books, 1964.

Judson, Karen. *Abraham Lincoln*. Springfield, N.J.: Enslow Publishers, Inc., 1998.

Kent, Zachary. *Andrew Johnson: Encyclopedia of Presidents*. Chicago: Children's Press, 1989.

Kennedy, John F. *Profiles in Courage*. New York: Harper and Row, 1964.

Milton, George Fort. *The Age of Hate: Andrew Johnson and the Radicals*. Hamden, Conn.: Archon Books, 1965.

Paley, Alan L. *Andrew Johnson: The President Impeached*. Charlotteville, N.Y.: SamHar Press, 1972.

Smith, Gene. *High Crimes and Misdemeanors: The Impeachment and Trial of Andrew Johnson*. New York: William Morrow and Co., Inc., 1977.

Steins, Richard. *Lincoln, Johnson, & Grant*. Vero Beach, Fla.: Rourke Corporation, 1996.

Stevens, Rita. *Andrew Johnson: Seventeenth President of the United States.* Ada, Okla.: Garrett Educational Corporation, 1989.

Thomas, Lately. *The First President Johnson.* New York: William Morrow and Co., Inc., 1968.

Trefousse, Hans L. *Andrew Johnson: A Biography.* New York: W. W. Norton and Co., 1989.

Winston, Robert W. *Andrew Johnson: Plebeian and Patriot.* New York: Barnes and Noble, 1969.

Places to Visit and Internet Addresses

Tennessee

Andrew Johnson National Historic Site, Greeneville. The park consists of Johnson's tailor shop, his two homes, and his burial ground and monument. Open year-round. (423) 638-3551.

For further research on Andrew Johnson:

Library of Congress
Web Site <http://www.loc.gov>

National Archives
Web Site <http://www.nara.gov>
E-mail <inquire@nara.gov>

National Park Service, Greeneville, Tennessee
Web Site <http://www.nps.gov/anjo>

The White House
Web Site <http://www.whitehouse.gov/WH/glimpse/presidents/html/aj17.html>

Index